Table of Contents

Introduction

Thai food can be, without a doubt, regarded as one of the tastiest and most sumptuous cuisines. Thai food became more popular in America when Thai restaurants became a popular thing in Los Angeles in the 1980s. Americans started to love green curry, Som Tam (green papaya salad), and Tom Yam (shrimp soup) remarkably. Irrespective of its familiarity with American society, Thai food can be considerably hard to prepare at home if you are a beginner.

Primarily, this is because the ingredients used in Thai dishes aren't that much familiar to American society. However, ingredients like fish sauce, fresh lime leaves, canned curry pastes, tamarind, and rice noodles are mostly available in non-Thai markets. But, the cooking techniques and orchestrating the dish effectively are mostly considered the weak areas for American cooks making Thai foods.

Moreover, another concern is having an exact and correct reference point while cooking a recipe. People who have been to Thailand certainly know a few recipes and dishes which they can prepare somewhat successfully after regular attempts. In case you haven't been to Thailand, you will be highly dependent on local North American Thai restaurants to teach you peculiar things like spicing levels, flavour balancing, serving individual dishes within meals, eaten as snacks, or solos, etc.

What is Thai Food?

Understanding Thai Food

Thai food is classified into four major categories, i.e., Northern, Northeastern (Isaan), Southern, and Central. They are defined and explained as below:

1. Northern

This food category includes the lush and cool valleys, mountains that are centred around Chiang Rai and Chiang Mai. It also shares its characteristics with northern Laos, Burma's Shan State, and the Chinese province of Yunnan.

2. Northeastern (Isaan)

This food category includes similarities with the cooking of Southern Laos across the Mekong River, some elements of Vietnamese cuisine, and some characteristic of the cuisines of the Cambodian region of Khmer.

3. Southern

This food category includes cuisines from Bangkok, covering the beautiful plains of the rice-growing central heartland. The mesmerizing refined court cooking of the ancient and famous Thai Kingdoms of Sukhothai and Ayutthaya.

4. Southern

This food category includes the cuisines from the beautiful Kra Isthmus, along with some characteristics of Indian, Indonesian, and Malaysian cuisines, including fresh turmeric and coconut milk.

The Chinese Influence on Thai Cuisine

Considerably, a large variety of Thai foods are considered to be direct adaptations of Chinese dishes. It is credited to the Hokkien immigrants who started living here in the early 15th century. Later on, a Thai-Chinese community merged with Teochew immigrants. The Wok cooking, deep-frying, soy sauce, noodle dishes, and taochiao (fermented bean paste) is credited to the Chinese cooks. Moreover, even the rice porridge or Thai breakfast chok is also associated with Chinese cooks, just like many other Thai dishes.

Enter the Chile

Surprisingly, chillies are considered one of the deeply fixed in the entire Thai culinary. However, it is essential to know that they were introduced in Thai cuisine in the 16th and 17th century when the Portuguese and the Spanish brought them after adopting them from Central America. Peanuts, papayas, tomatoes, eggplant, pumpkin, and pineapple was also adopted from America.

The Thai Street Food

There are two significant portions of Thai cuisine, i.e., food eaten with rice called Arharn Gap Hkao, which acts as the base of the meal proper. It covers a significant amount of Thai foods, including soups, relishes, curries, and salads. All of these foods are consumed with rice, which acts as the prime meal. The second principal component of Thai Cuisine is Arharn Jarn Dtiaw, i.e., single-plate food. It is basically just like that; the dish is usually plated in separate small portions. It was initially introduced in the markets and later on made its way to the streets. The main street foods are classified as noodles, complex desserts, pastries, braised and deep-fried dishes. These street foods can be easily prepared at home.

The Thai Food Cookbook

The Thai Food cookbook will provide you with a realistic and fantastic taste of Thai cuisine. It will provide comprehensive assistance in mastering the Thai cuisines and different recipes and foods of Thai origin. The recipes will be thoroughly devised with easily understandable steps to follow. The cookbook will empower you to become a fantastic chef and provide yourself and your loved ones with the magical touch of Thai food. The cookbook will offer various recipes for every occasion, including breakfast, lunch, dinner, desserts, beverages, and much more. Moreover, the ingredients used in the recipes are most readily available in any supermarket, so that cooking is much more convenient for you to keep you motivated and adopt a healthy lifestyle.

Exotic Thai Morning Meals

Thai Congee

Preparation Time: 15 minutes
Cooking Time: 1 hour 45 minutes
Servings: 6

Ingredients:

- 1 cup rice
- 1/8 pound ground pork
- 1 teaspoon fish sauce
- 1 egg
- ½ cup pork broth
- 1 clove garlic, diced
- Black pepper, to taste

Preparation:

1. Boil rice in a pan and cover the lid.
2. Let the mixture simmer for about 90 minutes until rice forms porridge like consistency. Stir occasionally.
3. Meanwhile, add fish sauce, garlic and ground pork in a large bowl. Mix well.
4. Make bite-sized meatballs out of the mixture and set aside for a while.
5. Now, add pork broth, black pepper and meatballs in the rice mixture and simmer for about 3 minutes.
6. Add eggs and poach until egg white is formed.
7. Take out the congee and serve.

Serving Suggestions: Top with scallion before serving.

Variation Tip: Fish sauce can be replaced with soy sauce.

Nutritional Information per Serving:

Calories: 141 | **Fat:** 1.4g|**Sat Fat:** 0.4g|**Carbohydrates:** 25g|**Fiber:** 0.4g|**Sugar:** 0.2g|**Protein:** 6.1g

Thai Omelet

Preparation Time: 5 minutes
Cooking Time: 2 minutes
Servings: 2

Ingredients:

- 2 eggs
- 2 tablespoons vegetable oil
- ¼ teaspoon fish sauce
- ½ green onion, chopped

Preparation:

1. Break eggs in a bowl and add in green onion and fish sauce. Whisk properly.
2. Meanwhile, heat vegetable oil in a pan and pour egg mixture in it.
3. Cook for about 2 minutes until egg is golden brown and take out.
4. Place the Thai omelet on steamed rice and serve.

Serving Suggestions: Serve with Sriracha sauce.

Variation Tip: You can add herbs to enhance taste.

Nutritional Information per Serving:

Calories: 185 | **Fat:** 18g|**Sat Fat:** 4g|**Carbohydrates:** 0.7g|**Fiber:** 0.1g|**Sugar:** 0.5g|**Protein:** 5.7g

Thai Grilled Pork

Preparation Time: 30 minutes
Cooking Time: 25 minutes
Servings: 6

Ingredients:

- ½ pound pork shoulder, cut into strips
- ½ lemongrass stalk, chopped
- 1½ tablespoons coconut milk
- ½ tablespoon light soy sauce
- 1 teaspoon vegetable oil
- 3 garlic cloves, peeled
- 1 tablespoon sugar
- 1 tablespoon fish sauce
- ½ tablespoon coriander stalk, roughly chopped

Preparation:

1. Add lemongrass, coconut milk, soy sauce, vegetable oil, garlic cloves, sugar, fish sauce and coriander stalk in a food processor.
2. Pulse until a paste is formed.
3. Marinade the pork strips with the paste and refrigerate overnight.
4. Thread the pork on the skewers and set the barbeque up for direct grilling.
5. When the coals are white, cook the skewers and turn frequently until pork strips are cooked and caramelized.
6. Serve and enjoy!

Serving Suggestions: Serve with some sauce.

Variation Tip: You can omit coriander stalk.

Nutritional Information per Serving:

Calories: 161 | **Fat:** 12.1g|**Sat Fat:** 6g|**Carbohydrates:** 4.7g|**Fiber:** 0.3g|**Sugar:** 3.4g|**Protein:** 9.6g

Thai Grilled Chicken

Preparation Time: 15 minutes
Cooking Time: 15 minutes
Servings: 3

Ingredients:

- ½ lemongrass stalk, chopped
- 1 shallot, chopped
- 1 tablespoon vegetable oil
- 2 tablespoons Thai thin soy sauce
- 1 tablespoon fish sauce
- 3 pounds chicken, cut into pieces
- ¼ cup cilantro, chopped
- 4 cloves garlic, chopped
- 1 tablespoon palm sugar
- 1 teaspoon Thai sweet soy sauce
- ¼ teaspoon turmeric powder
- Salt and black pepper, to taste

Preparation:

1. Add lemongrass stalk, shallot, vegetable oil, Thai thin soy sauce, fish sauce, cilantro, garlic, palm sugar, Thai sweet sauce, turmeric powder, salt and pepper in a food processor.
2. Pulse until a smooth mixture is formed.
3. Marinade the chicken pieces with the mixture and refrigerate.
4. Take out 1 to 2 hours before cooking and set aside.
5. Grill the chicken for about 15 minutes and take out.
6. Serve and enjoy!

Serving Suggestions: Serve with hot sauce.

Variation Tip: You can omit turmeric powder.

Nutritional Information per Serving:

Calories: 865 | **Fat:** 19g|**Sat Fat:** 4.8g|**Carbohydrates:** 31.1g|**Fiber:** 0.2g|**Sugar:** 5.2g|**Protein:** 134.1g

Thai Donuts

Preparation Time: 10 minutes
Cooking Time: 10 minutes
Servings: 2

Ingredients:

- 2 cups flour
- ¼ teaspoon baking soda
- 2 teaspoons active dry yeast
- 2 teaspoons sugar
- 1 cup water
- ½ teaspoon salt
- Oil, for frying

Preparation:

1. Combine flour, baking soda, yeast, sugar and salt in a large bowl. Mix well.
2. Slowly add in water and mix until dough is formed.
3. Knead the dough and cover it with a damp cloth.
4. Set aside for about 2 hours.
5. Make 2 inch sticks out of the dough and press them in the center.
6. Meanwhile, heat up cooking oil in a pan and add donuts in it.
7. Cook until golden brown and puffy and take out.
8. Serve and enjoy!

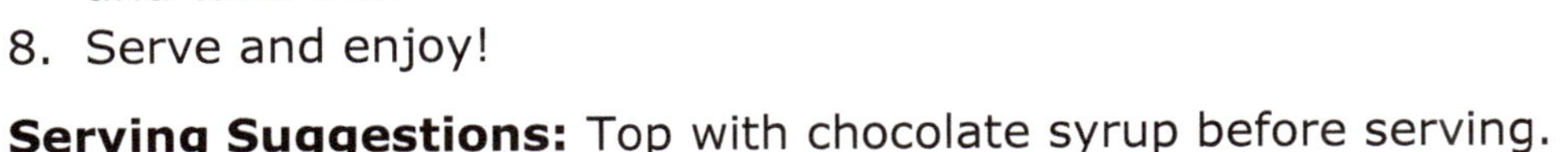

Serving Suggestions: Top with chocolate syrup before serving.

Variation Tip: Add cinnamon to enhance taste.

Nutritional Information per Serving:

Calories: 542 | **Fat:** 8.2g|**Sat Fat:** 1.1g|**Carbohydrates:** 100.9g|**Fiber:** 4.2g|**Sugar:** 4.3g|**Protein:** 14.4g

Thai Steamed Buns

Preparation Time: 30 minutes
Cooking Time: 15 minutes
Servings: 12

Ingredients:

- 3¾ cups all-purpose flour
- ¼ cup caster sugar
- 4 tablespoons dry yeast
- ¾ cup water
- 3 tablespoons butter
- 1½ pound minced pork
- ½ cup chopped spring onion
- 4 tablespoons oyster sauce
- 4 teaspoons sesame oil
- 4 garlic cloves
- 6 tablespoons soy sauce
- 2 teaspoons white pepper
- Pinch of salt

Preparation:

1. Add salt, flour, yeast and sugar in a bowl. Sift properly.
2. Set aside for about 10 minutes until yeast activates.
3. Now, add butter, activated yeast and water in the flour mixture.
4. Mix until the dough is formed and cover it with a damp cloth. Set aside for about 45 minutes.
5. Meanwhile, add minced pork, garlic, onion, soy sauce, oyster sauce, white pepper, and sesame oil in a large bowl.
6. Mix well and refrigerate for about one hour.
7. Now, take out the dough and divide it into 24 pieces.
8. Flatten the dough into circular shape and keep the edges thinner than the center.
9. Add the pork filling in the center of the dough and wrap the bun.
10. Repeat the process and cover the buns with a cloth for about 15 minutes before you steam them.
11. Steam for about 15 minutes and take out.
12. Serve and enjoy!

Serving Suggestions: Serve with green chili sauce.

Variation Tip: You can add ginger powder in pork mixture.

Nutritional Information per Serving:

Calories: 685 | **Fat:** 12.7g|**Sat Fat:** 4.7g|**Carbohydrates:** 72.9g|**Fiber:** 3.4g|**Sugar:** 4.7g|**Protein:** 65.6g

Thai Mango Sticky Rice

Preparation Time: 20 minutes
Cooking Time: 30 minutes
Servings: 20

Ingredients:

- 10 cups rice, boiled
- 5 cups coconut cream
- 1½ cups granulated sugar
- 10 cups mangoes, sliced
- 3 cups yellow mung beans
- Salt, to taste

Preparation:

1. Add half coconut cream, rice and sugar in a blender.
2. Blend until a smooth mixture is formed.
3. Meanwhile, add remaining coconut cream and salt in a pan and boil the mixture. Set aside.
4. Now, add beans in a frying pan and fry for few minutes and they become crispy.
5. Now, in a serving plate, add rice mixture and top it with coconut cream mixture, beans and sliced mangoes.
6. Serve and enjoy!

Serving Suggestions: Serve with maple syrup on the top.

Variation Tip: You can also use brown sugar.

Nutritional Information per Serving:

Calories: 830 | **Fat:** 15.4g|**Sat Fat:** 12.9g|**Carbohydrates:** 161.1g|**Fiber:** 10.7g| **Sugar:** 68.4g|**Protein:** 16.5g

Thai Waffles

Preparation Time: 10 minutes
Cooking Time: 15 minutes
Servings: 7

Ingredients:

- 2 tablespoons rice flour
- 3 tablespoons sugar
- 1 egg
- ¼ cup dried shrimp
- ½ cup all-purpose flour
- 6 tablespoons coconut milk
- ½ cup freshly squeezed lime juice

Preparation:

1. Grease a waffle iron and preheat it.
2. Meanwhile, add rice flour, sugar, egg, dried shrimp, all-purpose flour, coconut milk and lime juice in a large bowl.
3. Mix until a smooth batter is formed.
4. Pour the mixture in a waffle iron and cook for about 15 to 20 minutes.
5. Take out and serve.

Serving Suggestions: Serve with maple syrup on the top.

Variation Tip: You can also add coriander leaves to enhance taste.

Nutritional Information per Serving:

Calories: 105 | **Fat:** 3.9g|**Sat Fat:** 3g|**Carbohydrates:** 15.3g|**Fiber:** 0.6g|**Sugar:** 5.7g|**Protein:** 2.9g

Thai Fried Bananas

Preparation Time: 12 minutes
Cooking Time: 10 minutes
Servings: 10

Ingredients:

- 6 tablespoons white rice flour
- 1 tablespoon white sugar
- ¼ cup shredded coconut
- 5 bananas
- 2 tablespoons tapioca flour
- ½ cup water
- 1½ cups oil
- Salt, to taste

Preparation:

1. Add rice flour, sugar, shredded coconut, tapioca flour, and salt in a large bowl.
2. Add few drops of water at a time to form a thick batter. Mix well.
3. Cut bananas into 3 to 4 slices and cover them with the batter.
4. Meanwhile, heat up cooking oil in a frying pan and add bananas in it.
5. Fry until bananas turn golden and take out.
6. Serve and enjoy!

Serving Suggestions: Top it with honey before serving.

Variation Tip: Use powdered cinnamon on the top.

Nutritional Information per Serving:

Calories: 1214 | **Fat:** 120.8g|**Sat Fat:** 16.2g|**Carbohydrates:** 36.3g|**Fiber:** 2g|**Sugar:** 8.5g|**Protein:** 0.9g

Thai Soft-Boiled Eggs

Preparation Time: 7 minutes
Cooking Time: 5 minutes
Servings: 4

Ingredients:

- 4 eggs
- 1 large lime
- 2 shallots, chopped
- 2 tablespoons fish sauce
- 1 teaspoon sugar
- 2 tablespoons chili flakes
- Salt, to taste

Preparation:

1. Boil water in a pan and add eggs in it.
2. Simmer for about 5 minutes and take out the eggs. Set aside.
3. Meanwhile, add lime juice, fish sauce, sugar, shallots and chili flakes in a bowl. Mix well.
4. Now, cut eggs in half and top them with sauce.
5. Serve and enjoy!

Serving Suggestions: Garnish with coriander before serving.

Variation Tip: You can also add cayenne pepper to enhance taste.

Nutritional Information per Serving:

Calories: 79 | **Fat:** 4.4g|**Sat Fat:** 1.4g|**Carbohydrates:** 4.4g|**Fiber:** 0.5g|**Sugar:** 2g|**Protein:** 6.3g

Soups for Your Soul

Thai Chicken Soup

Preparation Time: 15 minutes
Cooking Time: 40 minutes
Servings: 3

Ingredients:

- ½ (4 pounds) chicken, cut into pieces
- 2 thin slices of fresh ginger
- 1 cup fresh cilantro
- 1 tablespoon lime juice
- ½ tablespoon fish sauce
- 4 cups water
- 2 garlic cloves, smashed
- 1½ shallots, thinly sliced
- 1 lemongrass stalk, chopped
- 1 fresh green Thai chili, thinly sliced
- Salt, to taste

Preparation:

1. Add chicken, water and salt in a large pan and boil it.
2. Now, add in ginger, garlic, shallots, lemongrass, cilantro, and lime juice. Stir well.
3. Lower the heat and simmer for about 30 minutes.
4. Strain the soup and discard the solids.
5. Now, return the soup in the skillet and add in chili and fish sauce.
6. Simmer for about 10 minutes and take out.
7. Serve and enjoy!

Serving Suggestions: Top with cilantro before serving.

Variation Tip: Fish sauce can be replaced with soy sauce.

Nutritional Information per Serving:

Calories: 129 | **Fat:** 1.5g|**Sat Fat:** 0.7g|**Carbohydrates:** 20g|**Fiber:** 0.6g|**Sugar:** 1.4g|**Protein:** 9g

Thai Red Curry Noodle Soup

Preparation Time: 10 minutes
Cooking Time: 20 minutes
Servings: 3

Ingredients:

- 1 tablespoon avocado oil
- ¼ cup diced red bell pepper
- 1½ garlic cloves, minced
- 2 tablespoons red curry paste
- 1 cup coconut milk
- ¼ cups rice noodles
- ¼ cup chopped cilantro
- ¼ cup diced yellow onion
- ¼ cup diced carrots
- ½ tablespoon freshly grated ginger
- 3 cups chicken broth
- 1½ tablespoons fish sauce
- ½ tablespoon fresh lime juice
- Salt and pepper, to taste

Preparation:

1. Heat up avocado oil in a Dutch oven and add red bell pepper, carrots and onions.
2. Cook for around 7 minutes and stir in red curry paste, ginger and garlic.
3. After 1 minute, add chicken broth, fish sauce and coconut milk. Stir well.
4. Add salt and pepper and cook for about 5 minutes.
5. Stir in noodles and simmer for about 7 minutes.
6. Take out and stir in lime juice and cilantro.
7. Serve and enjoy!

Serving Suggestions: Serve with soy sauce.

Variation Tip: You can also use vinegar to enhance taste.

Nutritional Information per Serving:

Calories: 320 | **Fat:** 24.2g|**Sat Fat:** 18.4g|**Carbohydrates:** 18.1g|**Fiber:** 3g|**Sugar:** 6.2g|**Protein:** 9.3g

Thai Coconut Soup

Preparation Time: 15 minutes
Cooking Time: 26 minutes
Servings: 4

Ingredients:

- ½ tablespoon vegetable oil
- ½ lemongrass stalk, minced
- 2 cups chicken broth
- ½ tablespoon brown sugar
- ¼ pound fresh shiitake mushrooms, sliced
- 1 tablespoon fresh lime juice
- 2 tablespoons fresh cilantro
- 1 tablespoon grated fresh ginger
- 1 teaspoon red curry paste
- 1½ tablespoons fish sauce
- 3 cups coconut milk
- ½ pound shrimp, peeled and deveined
- Salt, to taste

Preparation:

1. Heat up vegetable oil in a pan and add lemongrass, ginger, and curry paste.
2. Stir well and cook for about 1 minute.
3. Add in chicken broth, fish sauce and sugar.
4. Stir continuously and simmer for about 15 minutes.
5. Now, add mushrooms and coconut milk and cook for about 5 minutes.
6. Stir in shrimp and cook for about 5 more minutes.
7. Turn off the heat and stir in lemon juice and salt.
8. Garnish with cilantro and serve.

Serving Suggestions: Top with shredded coconut before serving.

Variation Tip: You can use chili sauce to enhance taste.

Nutritional Information per Serving:

Calories: 557 | **Fat:** 46.8g|**Sat Fat:** 39g|**Carbohydrates:** 19.5g|**Fiber:** 4.8g|**Sugar:** 9.6g|**Protein:** 21.3g

Vegan Thai Soup

Preparation Time: 10 minutes
Cooking Time: 15 minutes
Servings: 8

Ingredients:

- 1 red onion, chopped
- 6 mushrooms, sliced
- 1 inch piece of ginger, peeled and finely chopped
- 4 cups vegetable broth
- 2 tablespoons brown sugar
- 2 tablespoons soy sauce
- 1 red bell pepper, chopped
- 4 garlic cloves, chopped
- 1 Thai chili, finely chopped
- 3½ cups coconut milk
- 2½ cups firm tofu, cubed
- 2 tablespoons lime juice

Preparation:

1. Take a large pot and add Thai chili, ginger, garlic, mushrooms, red bell pepper, and onion in it.
2. Then add coconut milk, vegetable broth and sugar in the pot and mix well.
3. Boil the mixture and cook for about 5 minutes on medium heat.
4. Stir in tofu and cook for 5 more minutes.
5. Take out and stir in soy sauce and lime juice.
6. Serve and enjoy!

Serving Suggestions: Top with chopped cilantro before serving.

Variation Tip: Soy sauce can be replaced with tamari.

Nutritional Information per Serving:

Calories: 1393 | **Fat:** 126.1g|**Sat Fat:** 101.3g|**Carbohydrates:** 47.7g| **Fiber:** 14.1g|**Sugar:** 23.6g|**Protein:** 41.9g

Thai Shrimp Rice Soup

Preparation Time: 25 minutes
Cooking Time: 30 minutes
Servings: 8

Ingredients:

- 6 cups chicken stock
- ½ teaspoon white peppercorns
- ½ pound shrimp, cut into small chunks
- 1 tablespoon soy sauce
- 6 cups cooked jasmine rice
- 6 garlic cloves, minced
- 12 cilantro stems
- 2 tablespoons fish sauce

Preparation:

1. Add white peppercorns, garlic and cilantro in a food processor.
2. Pulse until a smooth puree is formed and marinade shrimps with half of the puree.
3. Sauté shrimps in a pan and add chicken stock in it.
4. Boil the stock and add remaining puree in it. Stir well.
5. Add in rice and cook for about 5 minutes.
6. Take out and stir in fish sauce and soy sauce.
7. Serve and enjoy!

Serving Suggestions: Top with coriander leaves before serving.

Variation Tip: Soy sauce can be omitted.

Nutritional Information per Serving:

Calories: 528 | **Fat:** 0.9g|**Sat Fat:** 0.3g|**Carbohydrates:** 110.3g|**Fiber:** 6.2g|**Sugar:** 0.8g|**Protein:** 16.6g

Thai Pork Noodle Soup

Preparation Time: 10 minutes
Cooking Time: 15 minutes
Servings: 8

Ingredients:

- 4 tablespoons canola oil
- 4 cups water
- 4 garlic cloves, chopped
- 2 pounds ground pork
- 2 tablespoons soy sauce
- 4 tablespoons fresh lime juice
- 4 scallions, thinly sliced
- 2 tablespoons fresh ginger, chopped
- 1 pound shiitake mushrooms
- 8 cups low-sodium chicken broth
- 8 cups wonton wrappers, sliced into ½ inch strips
- Salt, to taste

Preparation:

1. Put a pan on medium-high heat and add oil in it.
2. Sauté ginger, garlic and scallion and add in pork.
3. Cook for about 8 minutes and stir in mushrooms and salt.
4. Stir constantly for about 3 minutes and add in chicken broth, fish sauce and water.
5. Boil the mixture and stir in wonton wrappers.
6. Reduce the heat and simmer for about 2 minutes.
7. Add in lime juice and take out the soup.
8. Serve and enjoy!

Serving Suggestions: Serve with crackers.

Variation Tip: You can add vinegar to enhance taste.

Nutritional Information per Serving:

Calories: 380 | **Fat:** 11.7g|**Sat Fat:** 2g|**Carbohydrates:** 31.5g|**Fiber:** 2.3g|**Sugar:** 2.7g|**Protein:** 36.4g

Thai Pumpkin Coconut Soup

Preparation Time: 8 minutes
Cooking Time: 10 minutes
Servings: 1

Ingredients:

- 3 cups chicken stock
- 1 garlic clove, minced
- ½ red chili pepper, sliced
- 1 cup yam, chopped
- ½ teaspoon ground coriander
- 1 tablespoon fish sauce
- ½ teaspoon brown sugar
- ½ cup coconut milk
- 2 tablespoons lemongrass, minced
- ½ shallot, minced
- 1½ cups pumpkin, peeled and cut into chunks
- ¼ teaspoon turmeric
- ½ teaspoon ground cumin
- ½ teaspoon shrimp paste
- 1 tablespoon lime juice
- 1 cup soft tofu, cubed

Preparation:

1. Heat chicken stock in a pan and add garlic, chili, shallot and lemongrass in it.
2. Boil the mixture and add pumpkin and yam.
3. Cook for about 7 minutes and add spices. Stir well.
4. Let the mixture simmer for a while and add in coconut milk and tofu.
5. Take out and serve.

Serving Suggestions: You can serve with chopped cilantro on the top.

Variation Tip: You can also add spinach in the soup.

Nutritional Information per Serving:

Calories: 970 | **Fat:** 34.7g|**Sat Fat:** 27.9g|**Carbohydrates:** 166.3g|**Fiber:** 47.6g|
Sugar: 54.3g|**Protein:** 23.8g

Vegan Tom Yum Soup

Preparation Time: 10 minutes
Cooking Time: 15 minutes
Servings: 2

Ingredients:

- 3 cups vegetable stock
- 1 lime leaf
- 2 garlic cloves, minced
- ½ cup fresh mushrooms, sliced
- ½ cup cherry tomatoes
- ½ teaspoon brown sugar
- ½ tablespoon fresh lime juice
- 1 lemongrass stalk, minced
- ½ red chili, sliced
- ½ ginger, sliced
- 1 cup chopped bok choy leaves
- 1 tablespoon soy sauce
- 1 cup soft tofu, cubed

Preparation:

1. Heat vegetable stock in a pot and add lemongrass, lime leaf, ginger, garlic and chili in it. Stir well.
2. Boil the mixture and add mushrooms in it.
3. Simmer for about 8 minutes and add cherry tomatoes and bok choy. Stir properly.
4. Simmer for about 2 minutes and add in sugar, soy sauce and lime juice.
5. Stir in tofu and take out the soup.
6. Serve and enjoy!

Serving Suggestions: Top with chopped basil leaves before serving.

Variation Tip: Coconut milk can also be added in the soup.

Nutritional Information per Serving:

Calories: 150 | **Fat:** 5.5g|**Sat Fat:** 0.7g|**Carbohydrates:** 18.2g|**Fiber:** 4.9g|**Sugar:** 6.1g|**Protein:** 13.7g

Thai Vegetable Soup

Preparation Time: 20 minutes
Cooking Time: 30 minutes
Servings: 10

Ingredients:

- 3½ cups tofu, drained, pressed and sliced
- 2 carrots, chopped
- 4 tablespoons minced ginger
- 2 tablespoons minced garlic
- 8 cups vegetable broth
- 4 bok choy heads, roughly chopped
- 6 tablespoons extra-virgin olive oil
- 2 onions, finely chopped
- 2 red bell peppers, thinly sliced
- 3 cups chopped mushrooms
- 4 tablespoons curry powder
- 2 tablespoons lemongrass paste
- 8 cups coconut milk
- ½ cup chopped basil leaves
- Salt, to taste

Preparation:

1. Heat up olive oil in a pot and add tofu in it.
2. Cook for about 7 minutes, season with salt and take out. Set aside.
3. Now, add carrots, onions and peppers in the pot and cook for about 7 minutes. Stir well.
4. Add in mushrooms, curry powder, ginger, garlic, and lemongrass paste. Mix properly.
5. Cook for about 2 minutes and add coconut milk, bok choy, tofu and vegetable broth.
6. Simmer for about 15 minutes and take out.
7. Top with basil and serve.

Serving Suggestions: Serve with chopped mint leaves on the top.

Variation Tip: You can also use soy sauce to enhance taste.

Nutritional Information per Serving:

Calories: 908 | **Fat:** 72.9g|**Sat Fat:** 45.7g|**Carbohydrates:** 34.8g|**Fiber:** 13.6g|**Sugar:** 16.7g|**Protein:** 47.2g

Thai Butternut Squash Soup

Preparation Time: 20 minutes
Cooking Time: 25 minutes
Servings: 12

Ingredients:

- 4 tablespoons olive oil
- 2 yellow onions, chopped
- 6 tablespoons red curry paste
- 2 teaspoons ground cumin
- ¼ teaspoon red pepper flakes
- 8 cups vegetable broth
- 1 cup unsweetened coconut flakes
- 4 pounds butternut squash, cut into pieces
- 8 garlic cloves, chopped
- 4 teaspoons ground coriander
- 2 teaspoons lime juice
- Salt, to taste

Preparation:

1. Heat up olive-oil in a pan and add all the spices and vegetables in it.
2. Cook for about 8 minutes and stir in broth.
3. Simmer for about 20 minutes and add in coconut flakes. Stir well.
4. Take out and drizzle lime juice on the mixture.
5. Serve and enjoy!

Serving Suggestions: Garnish with red chili flakes before serving.

Variation Tip: Use oregano to enhance taste.

Nutritional Information per Serving:

Calories: 201 | **Fat:** 10.1g|**Sat Fat:** 3.4g|**Carbohydrates:** 24.3g|**Fiber:** 4.2g|**Sugar:** 4.7g|**Protein:** 5.5g

Thai Dishes from the Sea

Thai Fried Fish with Garlic and Sweet Chili Sauce

Preparation Time: 10 minutes
Cooking Time: 15 minutes
Servings: 2

Ingredients:

- 1 Nile Tilapia
- 1 Thai hot chili
- 1 tablespoon coconut sugar
- ½ cup vegetable oil
- ½ Thai long chili
- 2 garlic cloves
- 1 tablespoon fish sauce
- 1 tablespoon all-purpose flour

Preparation:

1. Coat fish with the flour and fry it for about 5 minutes on each side.
2. Take out and set aside.
3. Now, add garlic, hot chili, long chili, fish sauce and sugar in the pan and simmer it for around 5 minutes so the mixture becomes thick.
4. Pour the sauce on the fish and serve.

Serving Suggestions: Serve with steamed rice.

Variation Tip: You can also use honey in the sauce.

Nutritional Information per Serving:

Calories: 709 | **Fat:** 62.3g|**Sat Fat:** 12.2g|**Carbohydrates:** 25.6g|**Fiber:** 0.4g|**Sugar:** 1.1g|**Protein:** 11.8g

Thai Coconut Fish

Preparation Time: 15 minutes
Cooking Time: 20 minutes
Servings: 2

Ingredients:

- 1 tablespoon butter
- 1 tablespoon red curry paste
- 1 cup coconut milk
- 1 teaspoon finely chopped gingerroot
- 2 tablespoon finely chopped shallots
- 1 tablespoon fish sauce
- 1 tablespoon lemongrass, chopped
- ½ pound cod fillets, cut into chunks
- ¼ cup sweetened flaked coconut, toasted
- ½ teaspoon freshly grated lime zest
- ½ tablespoons chopped cilantro

Preparation:

1. Heat up butter in a skillet and add shallots in it.
2. Cook for around 5 minutes and add in curry paste.
3. Stir for about 1 minute and add in fish sauce, coconut milk, gingerroot and lemongrass.
4. Boil the mixture and let it simmer for about 6 minutes.
5. Add in cod and cook for about 7 minutes.
6. Take out and set aside.
7. Meanwhile, add sweetened coconut, cilantro and lime zest in a bowl. Mix well.
8. Pour the mixture on the cod and serve.

Serving Suggestions: Serve with chili flakes on the top.

Variation Tip: Add chili sauce to enhance taste.

Nutritional Information per Serving:

Calories: 497 | **Fat:** 41g|**Sat Fat:** 32.7g|**Carbohydrates:** 12.5g|**Fiber:** 3.6g|**Sugar:** 5g|**Protein:** 24.2g

Steamed Fish with Lime and Garlic

Preparation Time: 20 minutes
Cooking Time: 15 minutes
Servings: 2

Ingredients:

- 2 whole barramundi, guts and gills removed
- 10 lemongrass stalks, cut into chunks
- 2 cups fish stock
- 1 cup lime juice
- 4 garlic heads, chopped
- 30 sprigs cilantro, chopped
- 4 tablespoons palm sugar
- 12 tablespoons fish sauce
- Thai chilies, to taste

Preparation:

1. Stuff the lemongrass in fish cavity and steam the fish in boiling water for about 15 minutes.
2. Meanwhile, boil fish stock in a pan and add sugar in it. Stir well.
3. Take out the mixture when the sugar is completely dissolved in it and set aside.
4. Add fish sauce, lime juice, cilantro, chilies, and garlic in the stock and stir well.
5. Place the fish in serving plates and top with fish stock mixture.
6. Serve with steamed rice and enjoy!

Serving Suggestions: Garnish with chopped cilantro before serving.

Variation Tip: Chicken stock can be used instead of fish stock.

Nutritional Information per Serving:

Calories: 420 | **Fat:** 6.3g|**Sat Fat:** 0.5g|**Carbohydrates:** 46.5g|**Fiber:** 1.7g|**Sugar:** 13.7g|**Protein:** 49.9g

Thai Fish Curry

Preparation Time: 10 minutes
Cooking Time: 15 minutes
Servings: 8

Ingredients:

- 3 pounds white fish, cut into chunks
- 4 tablespoons coconut oil
- 4 tablespoons finely minced ginger
- 2 cups coconut milk
- 2 tablespoons fish sauce
- 6 tablespoons red curry paste
- 1 onion, finely chopped
- 6 garlic cloves, finely minced
- 1 cup water
- 2 tablespoons brown sugar
- 8 cups chopped vegetables

Preparation:

1. Marinade the fish with red curry paste and set aside.
2. Meanwhile, heat oil in a pot and add ginger, garlic and onion in it.
3. Cook for about 5 minutes and add in coconut milk, fish sauce, water and sugar. Stir well.
4. Now, stir in vegetables and boil the mixture.
5. Add fish in the mixture and cover the lid of the pot.
6. Cook for about 5 minutes and take out.
7. Serve and enjoy!

Serving Suggestions: Garnish with cilantro before serving.

Variation Tip: Black pepper can also be used to enhance taste.

Nutritional Information per Serving:

Calories: 579 | **Fat:** 29.7g|**Sat Fat:** 21.1g|**Carbohydrates:** 21g|**Fiber:** 5g|**Sugar:** 5g|**Protein:** 48.5g

Spicy Garlic Thai Shrimp

Preparation Time: 10 minutes
Cooking Time: 6 minutes
Servings: 2

Ingredients:

- ½ pound raw shrimp
- 1 tablespoon soy sauce
- 1 tablespoon honey
- ½ inch ginger, grated
- 2 tablespoons chopped onion
- 1 tablespoon sesame oil
- ½ tablespoons red pepper flakes
- 3 garlic cloves, minced

Preparation:

1. Add soy sauce, sesame oil, honey, red pepper flakes, ginger and garlic in a bowl. Mix well.
2. Add in shrimp and toss to coat well. Set aside.
3. Meanwhile, heat oil in a skillet and sauté onion in it.
4. Add in shrimp and cook for about 6 minutes.
5. Take out and serve.

Serving Suggestions: Top with hot sauce before serving.

Variation Tip: Replace sesame oil with olive oil.

Nutritional Information per Serving:

Calories: 248 | **Fat:** 9g|**Sat Fat:** 1.6g|**Carbohydrates:** 14.5g|**Fiber:** 0.8g|**Sugar:** 9.4g|**Protein:** 27g

Thai Shrimp and Basil Stir-Fry

Preparation Time: 15 minutes
Cooking Time: 2 minutes
Servings: 2

Ingredients:

- 1½ Thai chilies, coarsely chopped
- 2 tablespoons sugar
- ½ teaspoon kosher salt
- ½ pound large shrimp, peeled and deveined
- 3 garlic cloves, smashed
- 1 tablespoon fish sauce
- 2 tablespoons vegetable oil
- 1 cup basil leaves

Preparation:

1. Add garlic, sugar, chilies, fish sauce, salt and 1 tablespoon oil in a blender. Blend well.
2. Transfer the mixture in a bowl and add shrimp. Toss to coat well.
3. Set aside for 10 minutes and meanwhile, heat remaining oil in a skillet.
4. Add shrimps and cook for about 1 minute per side.
5. Take out the shrimps in a bowl and add basil.
6. Toss well until basil is wilted and transfer the mixture to serving plates.
7. Serve and enjoy!

Serving Suggestions: Serve with green chili sauce.

Variation Tip: Add a pinch of cayenne pepper to enhance taste.

Nutritional Information per Serving:

Calories: 956 | **Fat:** 27.5g|**Sat Fat:** 2.7g|**Carbohydrates:** 145.4g|**Fiber:** 3g|**Sugar:** 20.6g|**Protein:** 36.2g

Basil Prawns

Preparation Time: 10 minutes
Cooking Time: 15 minutes
Servings: 4

Ingredients:

- 16 prawns, trimmed and deveined
- 8 garlic cloves, peeled and sliced
- 2 cups basil leaves
- 2 teaspoons dark soy sauce
- 2 teaspoons sesame oil
- 4 tablespoons vegetable oil
- 2 red chilies, sliced
- 2 tablespoons soy sauce
- 4 teaspoons sugar
- 4 teaspoons cornstarch
- ½ cup water

Preparation:

1. Heat vegetable oil and chilies in a pan and add in prawns.
2. Fry for about 5 minutes and add soy sauce, dark soy sauce, sesame oil, sugar, and water. Mix well.
3. Stir in cornstarch and basil leaves and take out.
4. Serve and enjoy!

Serving Suggestions: Serve with steamed rice.

Variation Tip: You can also use white pepper to enhance taste.

Nutritional Information per Serving:

Calories: 340 | **Fat:** 17.5g|**Sat Fat:** 3.5g|**Carbohydrates:** 23.7g|**Fiber:** 0.5g|**Sugar:** 16.5g|**Protein:** 21.8g

Thai Green Prawn Curry

Preparation Time: 7 minutes
Cooking Time: 10 minutes
Servings: 2

Ingredients:

- 2 tablespoons sunflower oil
- 4 garlic cloves, finely chopped
- 1 cup coconut milk
- ¼ pound prawns, cooked
- 2 teaspoons lemon juice
- 2 shallots, finely chopped
- 4 tablespoons Thai green curry paste
- ¾ cups peas
- 2 teaspoons soy sauce

Preparation:

1. Heat up sunflower oil in a pan and add shallots and garlic in it.
2. Fry for about 2 minutes and add in coconut milk and green curry paste.
3. Cook for about 2 minutes and add in sugar and peas. Stir well.
4. Stir in lemon juice, soy sauce and prawns and cook for about 5 minutes.
5. Take out and serve.

Serving Suggestions: Serve with noodles.

Variation Tip: You can add chopped coriander to enhance taste.

Nutritional Information per Serving:

Calories: 841 | **Fat:** 68.5g|**Sat Fat:** 28.3g|**Carbohydrates:** 37.7g|**Fiber:** 15.6g|**Sugar:** 12.2g|**Protein:** 23.2g

Thai Lemongrass Baked Salmon

Preparation Time: 15 minutes
Cooking Time: 35 minutes
Servings: 2

Ingredients:

- 1 tablespoon dark soy sauce
- ½ lemongrass stalk, finely sliced
- ½ teaspoon fresh ginger, grated
- 1 tablespoon honey
- 2 tablespoons rice vinegar
- 1 shallot, diced
- ½ pound salmon fillets

Preparation:

1. Combine dark soy sauce and rice vinegar in a bowl. Set aside.
2. Combine ginger, lemongrass and shallot in another bowl. Set aside.
3. Now, cut shallow slits in salmon and cover it with ginger mixture.
4. Meanwhile, warm up the oven to 275 degrees F and place salmon in the baking oven.
5. Bake for about 35 minutes and take out.
6. Top with soy sauce mixture and serve.

Serving Suggestions: Serve with chopped coriander on the top.

Variation Tip: You can add lemon if you want.

Nutritional Information per Serving:

Calories: 251 | **Fat:** 7.1g|**Sat Fat:** 1g|**Carbohydrates:** 22.9g|**Fiber:** 0.1g|**Sugar:** 20.8g|**Protein:** 22.7g

Thai Salmon in Foil

Preparation Time: 5 minutes
Cooking Time: 20 minutes
Servings: 2

Ingredients:

- ¼ cup sweet chili sauce
- 1 garlic clove, minced
- ½ tablespoon freshly grated ginger
- 2 tablespoon peanuts, chopped
- 1 tablespoon reduced sodium soy sauce
- ½ tablespoon fish sauce
- 1 pound salmon
- 1 tablespoon fresh cilantro leaves

Preparation:

1. Heat up the oven to 375 degrees F and line the baking sheet with a foil.
2. Meanwhile, add chili sauce, fish sauce, soy sauce, ginger and garlic in a bowl. Mix well.
3. Place salmon on the baking dish and pour chili sauce on it.
4. Cover salmon with the foil and bake for about 20 minutes.
5. Take out and top with chopped peanuts.
6. Serve and enjoy!

Serving Suggestions: Serve chopped basil leaves on the top.

Variation Tip: You can also add dried oregano.

Nutritional Information per Serving:

Calories: 425 | **Fat:** 18.6g|**Sat Fat:** 2.7g|**Carbohydrates:** 15.9g|**Fiber:** 1.1g|**Sugar:** 12.7g|**Protein:** 47.3g

Exotic Thai Appetizers

Thai Chicken Lettuce Wraps

Preparation Time: 8 minutes
Cooking Time: 10 minutes
Servings: 2

Ingredients:

- 1 teaspoon olive oil
- 2 garlic cloves, minced
- ¼ teaspoon salt
- ½ carrot, shredded
- 1½ green onions, chopped
- ¼ pound chopped boneless, skinless chicken breasts
- ¼ cup yellow onion, chopped
- ¼ teaspoon black pepper
- ¼ cup cabbage, finely shredded
- ¼ cup sweet chili sauce
- ¼ teaspoon freshly grated ginger
- 2 tablespoons cilantro, chopped
- 1 head lettuce
- ½ tablespoon peanut butter
- 1 teaspoon low-sodium soy sauce

Preparation:

1. Heat-up olive oil in a skillet and add chicken, salt, pepper, garlic and onions in it. Cook and toss occasionally.
2. Add in carrots, green onions, and cabbage and cook for about 2 minutes.
3. Meanwhile, combine sweet chili sauce, peanut butter, ginger and soy sauce in a bowl.
4. Mix well and pour sauce in the pan.
5. Add cilantro and toss to coat well.
6. Take out and set the mixture in lettuce cups.
7. Serve and enjoy!

Serving Suggestions: Serve with chopped mint leaves on the top.

Variation Tip: Add red pepper flakes to enhance taste.

Nutritional Information per Serving:

Calories: 268 | **Fat:** 9g|**Sat Fat:** 1.9g|**Carbohydrates:** 25.6g|**Fiber:** 3.4g|**Sugar:** 16.8g|**Protein:** 19.7g

Thai Chicken Satay with Peanut Sauce

Preparation Time: 8 minutes
Cooking Time: 15 minutes
Servings: 7

Ingredients:

- 1 cup coconut milk
- ½ pound chicken thighs, chopped
- ½ teaspoon sugar
- ¼ cup peanut butter
- 1 teaspoon dark soy sauce
- 1 tablespoon cider vinegar
- ½ tablespoon curry powder
- 1 teaspoon red curry paste
- 2 tablespoons white sugar
- ½ cup water
- Salt, to taste

Preparation:

1. Combine chicken with ¼ cup coconut milk in a bowl. Mix well.
2. Thread 4 to 5 chicken pieces on each skewer and set aside.
3. Now, heat cooking oil in a pan and cook skewers for about 3 minutes on each side.
4. Meanwhile, add red curry paste, peanut butter, white sugar, soy sauce, salt, cider vinegar, and water in a bowl. Mix well.
5. Add remaining coconut milk and peanut butter mixture in a pan. Mix well.
6. Cook for about 5 minutes over medium-low heat and take out.
7. Pour the sauce on the skewers and serve.

Serving Suggestions: Serve with chopped peanuts on the top.

Variation Tip: Almond milk can be used instead of coconut milk.

Nutritional Information per Serving:

Calories: 218 | **Fat:** 15.5g|**Sat Fat:** 9g|**Carbohydrates:** 8.7g|**Fiber:** 1.5g|**Sugar:** 5.8g|**Protein:** 12.7g

Thai Spring Rolls

Preparation Time: 30 minutes
Servings: 12

Ingredients:

- 24 small, round rice wrappers, dried
- 2 tablespoons rice vinegar
- 2 teaspoons brown sugar
- 2 cups cooked shrimp
- 1 cup fresh Thai basil, roughly chopped
- 2 tablespoons shredded carrot
- 4 tablespoons soy sauce
- 2 tablespoons fish sauce
- 3 cups rice noodles, cooked
- 4 cups bean sprouts
- 1 cup fresh coriander, roughly chopped
- 6 onions, chopped

Preparation:

1. Add soy sauce, vinegar, brown sugar and fish sauce in a cup. Stir well.
2. Meanwhile, add rice, shrimp, noodles, bean sprouts, basil, carrots, coriander, and spring onions in a bowl. Mix well.
3. Add soy sauce mixture in shrimp mixture and toss to coat well.
4. Now, fill a large bowl with warm water and submerge rice wrappers in it for about 30 seconds each.
5. Take out the wrapper and add a spoonful of shrimp mixture on it.
6. Spread the mixture and fold the sides.
7. Serve and enjoy!

Serving Suggestions: Serve with tamarind sauce.

Variation Tip: Use Roman coriander for an even better taste.

Nutritional Information per Serving:

Calories: 207 | **Fat:** 1.1g|**Sat Fat:** 0.2g|**Carbohydrates:** 40.7g|**Fiber:** 2.4g|**Sugar:** 3.9g|**Protein:** 8.8g

Thai Corn Fritters

Preparation Time: 10 minutes
Cooking Time: 4 minutes
Servings: 8

Ingredients:

- 4 cups fresh corn kernels
- 6 green onions, thinly sliced
- 6 tablespoons coconut milk
- 2 teaspoons chili garlic sauce
- ½ cup all-purpose flour
- 2 teaspoons baking powder
- ½ cup cilantro, chopped
- 2 eggs
- 4 teaspoons ginger, finely minced
- 4 tablespoons coconut oil
- Salt and pepper, to taste

Preparation:

1. Combine corn, cilantro, green onions, coconut milk, eggs, ginger, and chili garlic sauce in a bowl. Mix well.
2. Add in salt, pepper, all-purpose flour, and baking powder. Sift properly.
3. Heat-up coconut oil in a skillet and add corn mixture in it.
4. Flatten the top and cook for about 2 minutes on each side.
5. Take out and serve.

Serving Suggestions: Serve with a dipping sauce.

Variation Tip: You can add red curry paste to enhance taste.

Nutritional Information per Serving:

Calories: 215 | **Fat:** 11.9g|**Sat Fat:** 8.8g|**Carbohydrates:** 25.8g|**Fiber:** 3.3g|**Sugar:** 4.8g|**Protein:** 5.8g

Supreme Thai Ribs

Preparation Time: 12 minutes
Cooking Time: 2 hours
Servings: 4

Ingredients:

- 4 tablespoons onion, minced
- 2 green chilies, minced
- 4 tablespoons fish sauce
- ½ cup brown sugar
- 4 tablespoons cornstarch
- 6 garlic cloves, minced
- ½ cup soy sauce
- 4 teaspoons rice vinegar
- 8 tablespoons maple syrup
- 4 pounds pork ribs

Preparation:

1. Combine garlic, onion, chilies, soy sauce, rice vinegar, fish sauce, maple syrup and brown sugar in a bowl. Mix well.
2. Add in cornstarch, whisk well and set aside.
3. Meanwhile, place the ribs in a tray and pour soy sauce mixture on it.
4. Place it in refrigerator for about 24 hours.
5. Now, preheat the oven to 275 degrees F and bake the ribs for about 2 hours.
6. Take out and serve.

Serving Suggestions: Serve with steamed rice.

Variation Tip: You can also use chili sauce to enhance taste.

Nutritional Information per Serving:

Calories: 1052 | **Fat:** 52.8g|**Sat Fat:** 20.2g|**Carbohydrates:** 57.6g|**Fiber:** 0.7g|**Sugar:** 43.2g|**Protein:** 84.4g

Thai Dragon Fruit Vodka Cocktail

Preparation Time: 10 minutes
Servings: 4

Ingredients:

- 2 cups dragon fruit
- 2 teaspoons honey
- ¾ cup vodka
- 4 limes
- 2 blood oranges
- ¼ cup orange liquor

Preparation:

1. Add dragon fruit, lime juice, and blood orange in a blender.
2. Blender until a smooth mixture is formed.
3. Add in honey, vodka and orange liquor. Blend properly.
4. Take out and top with crushed ice.
5. Serve and enjoy!

Serving Suggestions: Top with mint leaves before serving.

Variation Tip: Maple syrup can be used instead of honey.

Nutritional Information per Serving:

Calories: 204 | **Fat:** 1.2g|**Sat Fat:** 0.6g|**Carbohydrates:** 27.2 |**Fiber:** 4.4g|**Sugar:** 18.6g|**Protein:** 1.6g

Supreme Thai Ribs

Preparation Time: 12 minutes
Cooking Time: 2 hours
Servings: 4

Ingredients:

- 4 tablespoons onion, minced
- 2 green chilies, minced
- 4 tablespoons fish sauce
- ½ cup brown sugar
- 4 tablespoons cornstarch
- 6 garlic cloves, minced
- ½ cup soy sauce
- 4 teaspoons rice vinegar
- 8 tablespoons maple syrup
- 4 pounds pork ribs

Preparation:

1. Combine garlic, onion, chilies, soy sauce, rice vinegar, fish sauce, maple syrup and brown sugar in a bowl. Mix well.
2. Add in cornstarch, whisk well and set aside.
3. Meanwhile, place the ribs in a tray and pour soy sauce mixture on it.
4. Place it in refrigerator for about 24 hours.
5. Now, preheat the oven to 275 degrees F and bake the ribs for about 2 hours.
6. Take out and serve.

Serving Suggestions: Serve with steamed rice.

Variation Tip: You can also use chili sauce to enhance taste.

Nutritional Information per Serving:

Calories: 1052 | **Fat:** 52.8g|**Sat Fat:** 20.2g|**Carbohydrates:** 57.6g|**Fiber:** 0.7g|**Sugar:** 43.2g|**Protein:** 84.4g

7. Pour the mixture on popcorns and serve.

Serving Suggestions: Garnish cilantro on the top before serving.

Variation Tip: You can add some grated ginger for additional flavor.

Nutritional Information per Serving:

Calories: 461 | **Fat:** 31.8g|**Sat Fat:** 3.9g|**Carbohydrates:** 40.2g|**Fiber:** 3.4g|**Sugar:** 34g|**Protein:** 9.9g

Thai Pinwheels with Peanut Sauce

Preparation Time: 15 minutes
Servings: 12

Ingredients:

- 2 tortillas
- 4 tablespoons grated carrot
- 1 avocado, sliced
- 6 tablespoons cilantro
- 1 fresh red pepper
- 1 cup peanut butter
- 1 teaspoon sriracha
- 2 teaspoons brown rice vinegar
- ½ cup sweet red chili sauce
- 1 teaspoon tamari
- 2 tablespoons lime juice

Thai Dragon Fruit Vodka Cocktail

Preparation Time: 10 minutes
Servings: 4

Ingredients:

- 2 cups dragon fruit
- 2 teaspoons honey
- ¾ cup vodka
- 4 limes
- 2 blood oranges
- ¼ cup orange liquor

Preparation:

1. Add dragon fruit, lime juice, and blood orange in a blender.
2. Blender until a smooth mixture is formed.
3. Add in honey, vodka and orange liquor. Blend properly.
4. Take out and top with crushed ice.
5. Serve and enjoy!

Serving Suggestions: Top with mint leaves before serving.

Variation Tip: Maple syrup can be used instead of honey.

Nutritional Information per Serving:

Calories: 204 | **Fat:** 1.2g|**Sat Fat:** 0.6g|**Carbohydrates:** 27.2 |**Fiber:** 4.4g|**Sugar:** 18.6g|**Protein:** 1.6g

Supreme Thai Ribs

Preparation Time: 12 minutes
Cooking Time: 2 hours
Servings: 4

Ingredients:

- 4 tablespoons onion, minced
- 2 green chilies, minced
- 4 tablespoons fish sauce
- ½ cup brown sugar
- 4 tablespoons cornstarch
- 6 garlic cloves, minced
- ½ cup soy sauce
- 4 teaspoons rice vinegar
- 8 tablespoons maple syrup
- 4 pounds pork ribs

Preparation:

1. Combine garlic, onion, chilies, soy sauce, rice vinegar, fish sauce, maple syrup and brown sugar in a bowl. Mix well.
2. Add in cornstarch, whisk well and set aside.
3. Meanwhile, place the ribs in a tray and pour soy sauce mixture on it.
4. Place it in refrigerator for about 24 hours.
5. Now, preheat the oven to 275 degrees F and bake the ribs for about 2 hours.
6. Take out and serve.

Serving Suggestions: Serve with steamed rice.

Variation Tip: You can also use chili sauce to enhance taste.

Nutritional Information per Serving:

Calories: 1052 | **Fat:** 52.8g|**Sat Fat:** 20.2g|**Carbohydrates:** 57.6g|**Fiber:** 0.7g|**Sugar:** 43.2g|**Protein:** 84.4g

Thai Pinwheels with Peanut Sauce

Preparation Time: 15 minutes
Servings: 12

Ingredients:

- 2 tortillas
- 4 tablespoons grated carrot
- 1 avocado, sliced
- 6 tablespoons cilantro
- 1 fresh red pepper
- 1 cup peanut butter
- 1 teaspoon sriracha
- 2 teaspoons brown rice vinegar
- ½ cup sweet red chili sauce
- 1 teaspoon tamari
- 2 tablespoons lime juice

Preparation:

1. Add peanut butter, sweet red chili sauce, sriracha, tamari, brown rice vinegar, and lime juice in a bowl. Mix well.
2. Spread cilantro, avocado, red pepper, peanut sauce and carrot on tortilla.
3. Roll tightly and slice with a knife.
4. Serve and enjoy!

Serving Suggestions: Garnish with chopped mint leaves before serving.

Variation Tip: You can omit sriracha.

Nutritional Information per Serving:

Calories: 197 | **Fat:** 14.2g|**Sat Fat:** 3g|**Carbohydrates:** 13.9g|**Fiber:** 2.9g|**Sugar:** 6.9g|**Protein:** 6.1g

Thai Style Popcorn

Preparation Time: 12 minutes
Cooking Time: 15 minutes
Servings: 12

Ingredients:

- 4 tablespoons olive oil
- 3 cups salted peanuts, roughly chopped
- 1 cup un-popped popcorns
- ½ cup almond oil
- 4 tablespoons soy sauce
- 2 tablespoons lime zest
- ½ teaspoon baking soda
- 1¼ cups brown sugar
- 6 tablespoons sriracha sauce
- 2 tablespoons lime juice

Preparation:

1. Add olive oil and un-popped popcorn kernels in a large pan.
2. Stir well and cover the lid of the pan.
3. Cook for about 10 minutes until all the popcorn kernels are popped.
4. Meanwhile, add brown sugar, almond oil, soy sauce, lime juice, sriracha, and lime zest in a pan. Mix well.
5. Simmer for about 5 minutes and take out.
6. Add in baking soda and mix well.
7. Pour the mixture on popcorns and serve.

Serving Suggestions: Garnish cilantro on the top before serving.

Variation Tip: You can add some grated ginger for additional flavor.

Nutritional Information per Serving:

Calories: 461 | **Fat:** 31.8g|**Sat Fat:** 3.9g|**Carbohydrates:** 40.2g|**Fiber:** 3.4g|**Sugar:** 34g|**Protein:** 9.9g

Thai Dragon Fruit Vodka Cocktail

Preparation Time: 10 minutes
Servings: 4

Ingredients:

- 2 cups dragon fruit
- 2 teaspoons honey
- ¾ cup vodka
- 4 limes
- 2 blood oranges
- ¼ cup orange liquor

Preparation:

1. Add dragon fruit, lime juice, and blood orange in a blender.
2. Blender until a smooth mixture is formed.
3. Add in honey, vodka and orange liquor. Blend properly.
4. Take out and top with crushed ice.
5. Serve and enjoy!

Serving Suggestions: Top with mint leaves before serving.

Variation Tip: Maple syrup can be used instead of honey.

Nutritional Information per Serving:

Calories: 204 | **Fat:** 1.2g|**Sat Fat:** 0.6g|**Carbohydrates:** 27.2 |**Fiber:** 4.4g|**Sugar:** 18.6g|**Protein:** 1.6g

Thai Fruit Skewers

Preparation Time: 15 minutes
Servings: 16

Ingredients:

- 1 cup reduced-fat coconut milk
- ¼ teaspoon cayenne pepper
- 8 pineapple pieces
- 8 mango slices
- 8 papaya slices
- ½ cup shredded coconut, toasted
- 2 tablespoons finely shredded lime peel
- 4 kiwis, peeled and quartered
- ½ cup fresh mint

Preparation:

1. Add coconut milk, cayenne pepper and lime peel in a bowl. Mix well.
2. Add in kiwi, pineapple, papaya and mango. Toss to coat well.
3. Cover for about 4 hours and strain the mixture.
4. Thread fruits alternately on skewers and sprinkle with coconut and mint.
5. Serve and enjoy!

Serving Suggestions: Serve with honey on the top.

Variation Tip: You can also add chia seeds in the mixture.

Nutritional Information per Serving:

Calories: 180 | **Fat:** 5.2g|**Sat Fat:** 4.1g|**Carbohydrates:** 36.2g|**Fiber:** 5.3g|**Sugar:** 27.6g|**Protein:** 2.3g

Sweet and Spicy Thai Cashews

Preparation Time: 15 minutes
Cooking Time: 20 minutes
Servings: 4

Ingredients:

- 2 tablespoons coconut oil
- 4 teaspoons Thai red curry paste
- 2 teaspoons ground coriander
- ½ teaspoon ground turmeric
- 2 tablespoons coconut palm sugar
- 4 tablespoons raw sesame seeds
- 4 tablespoons honey
- 2 teaspoons lime juice
- 1 teaspoon ground ginger
- ¼ teaspoon ground cayenne
- 4 cups raw cashews
- Salt, to taste

Preparation:

1. Warm up the baking oven to 350 degrees F and line a baking sheet with parchment paper.
2. Meanwhile, add coconut oil, honey, red curry paste, ginger, lime juice, coriander, and turmeric in a bowl. Mix well.
3. Add in cayenne pepper, sugar, salt and sesame seeds. Stir well.
4. Add cashews in the bowl and toss to coat well.
5. Place cashews on the baking sheet and bake for about 20 minutes.
6. Take out and serve.

Serving Suggestions: Garnish with chopped mint leaves before serving.

Variation Tip: Turmeric can be omitted.

Nutritional Information per Serving:

Calories: 1011 | **Fat:** 76.3g|**Sat Fat:** 19.6g|**Carbohydrates:** 73.6g|**Fiber:** 5.4g|**Sugar:** 29g|**Protein:** 22.8g

Desirable Desserts

Thai Mango Coconut Pudding

Preparation Time: 15 minutes
Servings: 10

Ingredients:

- 4 mangoes
- 1 cup water
- ½ cup white sugar
- 1½ cups coconut milk
- 4 tablespoons gelatin powder

Preparation:

1. Add mangoes in a food processor and pulse until a smooth puree is formed.
2. Transfer the puree in a bowl and add coconut milk. Stir well.
3. Add boiled water, gelatin and sugar in a bowl. Stir well.
4. Combine mango and gelatin mixtures and mix properly.
5. Pour the mixture in serving glasses and refrigerate.
6. Serve and enjoy!

Serving Suggestions: Top it with whipped cream before serving.

Variation Tip: Coconut sugar can also be used.

Nutritional Information per Serving:

Calories: 431 | **Fat:** 32g|**Sat Fat:** 28g|**Carbohydrates:** 37.4g|**Fiber:** 5.1g|**Sugar:** 32.8g|**Protein:** 6.5g

Thai Banana in Coconut Milk

Preparation Time: 10 minutes
Cooking Time: 10 minutes
Servings: 4

Ingredients:

- 3 cups coconut milk
- 2 tablespoons sugar
- 4 bananas, sliced
- Salt, to taste

Preparation:

1. Boil coconut milk in a saucepan and add banana slices in it.
2. Reduce the heat and simmer for about 5 minutes.
3. Stir in sugar and salt and take out.
4. Serve and enjoy!

Serving Suggestions: Top with shredded coconut before serving.

Variation Tip: You can also add honey to enhance taste.

Nutritional Information per Serving:

Calories: 542 | **Fat:** 43.3g|**Sat Fat:** 38.2g|**Carbohydrates:** 42.9g|**Fiber:** 7g|**Sugar:** 26.4g|**Protein:** 5.4g

Strawberry Cheesecake Rolled Ice cream

Preparation Time: 10 minutes
Cooking Time: 4 minutes
Servings: 4

Ingredients:

- 2 cups cream
- 6 strawberries, diced
- 4 tablespoons cream cheese
- 1 cup condensed milk
- 4 tablespoons crushed graham crackers

Preparation:

1. In a large baking tray, add condensed milk and cream. Mix well.
2. Then, add cream cheese, strawberries and graham crackers.
3. Break all the ingredients into small chunks until mixture is well combined.
4. Place the tray in the freezer overnight or for at least 6 hours.
5. Take out and with the help of offset spatula, roll the ice cream into itself to form a spiral shape.
6. Top with whipped cream and serve.

Serving Suggestions: Serve with strawberry slices on the top.

Variation Tip: You can also add strawberry syrup for an even better taste.

Nutritional Information per Serving:

Calories: 386 | **Fat:** 17.4g|**Sat Fat:** 10.6g|**Carbohydrates:** 51.1g|**Fiber:** 0.5g|**Sugar:** 46.6g|**Protein:** 8.3g

Banana Spring Rolls

Preparation Time: 10 minutes
Cooking Time: 4 minutes
Servings: 6

Ingredients:

- 6 spring roll wrappers
- 3 tablespoons palm sugar
- 1½ tablespoons butter
- 3 bananas, halved
- 1½ tablespoons oil

Preparation:

1. Add half banana and ½ tablespoon sugar in each wrapper and seal it with water.
2. Add butter and oil in a pan and fry spring rolls for 2 minutes per side.
3. Take out and serve.

Serving Suggestions: Top with icing sugar before serving.

Variation Tip: You can add some cinnamon too.

Nutritional Information per Serving:

Calories: 357 | **Fat:** 23.7|**Sat Fat:** 8.5g|**Carbohydrates:** 34g|**Fiber:** 2.1g|**Sugar:** 9.1g|**Protein:** 3.9g

Thai Steamed Banana Cake

Preparation Time: 5 minutes
Cooking Time: 30 minutes
Servings: 2

Ingredients:

- 1 banana
- 1 tablespoon potato flour
- ½ cup grated coconut meat
- ¼ cup rice flour
- ½ cup sugar
- ¼ cup coconut milk

Preparation:

1. Mash banana in a bowl and add sugar, coconut cream, rice flour, coconut flour and grated coconut meat. Mix well.
2. Pour the batter in a cake mould and steam for about 30 minutes.
3. Take out and top with grated coconut meat.
4. Serve and enjoy!

Serving Suggestions: Top with banana slices before serving.

Variation Tip: You can also add honey to enhance taste.

Nutritional Information per Serving:

Calories: 470 | **Fat:** 14.3g|**Sat Fat:** 12.4g|**Carbohydrates:** 88.2g|**Fiber:** 4.8g|**Sugar:** 59.7g|**Protein:** 3.5g

Thai Grilled Pineapples

Preparation Time: 5 minutes
Cooking Time: 6 minutes
Servings: 2

Ingredients:

- ½ pineapple, sliced
- 1½ tablespoons butter
- 1 tablespoon palm sugar
- ½ tablespoon coconut, grated
- 1½ tablespoons lemon juice

Preparation:

1. Melt butter in a pan and add pineapple slices in it.
2. Top with palm sugar and lemon juice and cook for about 3 minutes on each side.
3. Take out and top with coconut.
4. Serve and enjoy!

Serving Suggestions: Serve with steamed rice.

Variation Tip: Pineapple juice can be used instead of lemon juice.

Nutritional Information per Serving:

Calories: 323 | **Fat:** 32.5g|**Sat Fat:** 20.8g|**Carbohydrates:** 8.5g|**Fiber:** 0.9g|**Sugar:** 6.9g|**Protein:** 0.9g

Thai Coconut Pudding

Preparation Time: 10 minutes
Cooking Time: 35 minutes
Servings: 6

Ingredients:

- 4 eggs
- 1 teaspoon vanilla essence
- ¾ tablespoons brown sugar
- 1 tablespoon all-purpose flour
- ½ cup grated coconut
- 1 cup coconut milk
- Icing sugar, to taste

Preparation:

1. Preheat the baking oven to 260 degrees F and grease a baking dish.
2. Meanwhile, add sugar and eggs in a large bowl. Whisk well.
3. Add in coconut milk, grated coconut and vanilla essence. Whisk again.
4. Pour the mixture in a baking-dish and bake for about 35 minutes.
5. Take out and top with icing sugar.
6. Serve and enjoy!

Serving Suggestions: Top with whipped cream before serving.

Variation Tip: You can use coconut sugar instead of brown sugar.

Nutritional Information per Serving:

Calories: 174 | **Fat:** 14.7g|**Sat Fat:** 11.3g|**Carbohydrates:** 7g|**Fiber:** 1.5g|**Sugar:** 4.5g|**Protein:** 5g

Thai Mango Cake

Preparation Time: 5 minutes
Cooking Time: 30 minutes
Servings: 4

Ingredients:

- 3 eggs
- ½ tablespoon sweetened dried coconut
- 1 teaspoon baking powder
- 1 tablespoon coconut oil
- 1 cup diced mangoes
- ½ cup sugar
- ½ cup all-purpose flour
- ½ teaspoon vanilla extract
- 1/8 teaspoon salt

Preparation:

1. Warm up the baking oven to 325 degrees F and grease a cake pan.
2. Meanwhile, add eggs and sugar in a large bowl. Whisk well.
3. Add in baking powder, flour, coconut oil, vanilla essence and salt. Beat well.
4. Now, add half cup of mangoes in a blender and blend until a puree is formed.
5. Pour the puree in the batter and beat again.
6. Add the mixture in the pan and bake for about 30 minutes.
7. Take out and top with dried coconut and mango slices.
8. Serve and enjoy!

Serving Suggestions: Add whipped cream on the top before serving.

Variation Tip: Vanilla extract can be replaced with coconut extract.

Nutritional Information per Serving:

Calories: 278 | **Fat:** 9.3g|**Sat Fat:** 6.1g|**Carbohydrates:** 44.9g|**Fiber:** 1.7g|**Sugar:** 31.3g|**Protein:** 6.3g

Thai Shaved Ice Dessert

Preparation Time: 10 minutes
Servings: 2

Ingredients:

- 2 tablespoons basil seeds, soaked
- 1½ tablespoons croutons
- 2 teaspoons condensed milk
- 2 cups shaved ice
- 6 tablespoons raspberry syrup

Preparation:

1. Take a dessert bowl and place a layer of basil seeds, ice and croutons.
2. Top the dessert with syrup and condensed milk.
3. Serve and enjoy!

Serving Suggestions: Top with raspberries before serving.

Variation Tip: You can also use blueberry syrup.

Nutritional Information per Serving:

Calories: 374 | **Fat:** 15.1g|**Sat Fat:** 11.4g|**Carbohydrates:** 59.5g|**Fiber:** 1g|**Sugar:** 51.5g|**Protein:** 3.9g

Thai Mango Ice cream

Preparation Time: 15 minutes
Servings: 12

Ingredients:

- 4 mangoes, sliced
- 6 tablespoons coconut milk
- 2 cups whipping cream
- 2 cups white sugar
- 2 teaspoons lemon juice

Preparation:

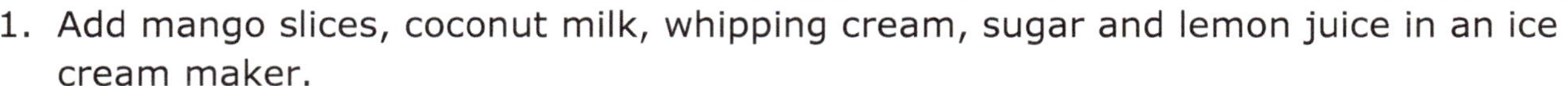

1. Add mango slices, coconut milk, whipping cream, sugar and lemon juice in an ice cream maker.
2. Process the ice cream maker according to manufacturer's instructions and pour the mixture in an airtight container.
3. Place the container in a freezer for about 8 hours and take out.
4. Serve and enjoy!

Serving Suggestions: Top with mango slices before serving.

Variation Tip: Almond milk can be used instead of coconut milk.

Nutritional Information per Serving:

Calories: 268 | **Fat:** 8.4g|**Sat Fat:** 5.6g|**Carbohydrates:** 51.1g|**Fiber:** 2g|**Sugar:** 48.9g|**Protein:** 1.5g

Inspiring Thai Vegetables and Salads

Thai Stir-Fried Bok Choy

Preparation Time: 7 minutes
Cooking Time: 5 minutes
Servings: 2

Ingredients:

- 1 large bok choy head, chopped
- 2 garlic cloves, minced
- 1 tablespoon soy sauce
- 1 tablespoon sweet chili sauce
- 1 tablespoon lime juice
- ½ tablespoon coconut oil
- 1 tablespoon oyster-flavored sauce
- 1 tablespoon fish sauce
- 1 tablespoon brown sugar

Preparation:

1. Add garlic cloves, soy sauce, sweet chili sauce, lime juice, oyster-flavored sauce, fish sauce, and brown sugar in a bowl. Mix well.
2. Heat up coconut oil in a frying-pan and add bok choy in it.
3. Pour soy sauce mixture in the pan and stir continuously.
4. Fry for about 5 minutes and take out.
5. Serve and enjoy!

Serving Suggestions: Squeeze lemon before serving.

Variation Tip: Fish sauce can be omitted.

Nutritional Information per Serving:

Calories: 116 | **Fat:** 3.9g|**Sat Fat:** 2.9g|**Carbohydrates:** 18.2g|**Fiber:** 2.2g|**Sugar:** 11.8g|**Protein:** 4.8g

Thai Stir-Fried Broccoli

Preparation Time: 5 minutes
Cooking Time: 6 minutes
Servings: 1

Ingredients:

- 6 broccoli stalks
- ¼ teaspoon dried crushed chili
- 1½ tablespoons sherry
- ¾ tablespoon oyster sauce
- ¾ tablespoon chopped garlic
- 1½ tablespoons vegetable oil
- 2 tablespoons chicken stock
- 1 teaspoon brown sugar

Preparation:

1. Add oyster sauce, sherry, brown sugar and chicken stock in a cup. Mix well.
2. Meanwhile, heat up vegetable oil in a pan and add garlic and chili in it.
3. Cook for about 1 minute and add broccoli and sherry mixture. Stir well.
4. Cook for about 5 minutes and take out.
5. Serve and enjoy!

Serving Suggestions: Garnish it with chopped mint leaves before serving.

Variation Tip: You can also add sriracha sauce to enhance taste.

Nutritional Information per Serving:

Calories: 1217 | **Fat:** 76.7g|**Sat Fat:** 14.7g|**Carbohydrates:** 51.4g|**Fiber:** 14.8g| **Sugar:** 17.3g|**Protein:** 16.3g

Thai Baked Sweet Potatoes and Purple Yams

Preparation Time: 5 minutes
Cooking Time: 45 minutes
Servings: 2

Ingredients:

- 1 sweet potato, peeled and cubed
- ½ carrot, chopped
- ¼ teaspoon cayenne pepper
- ½ teaspoon cumin seeds
- 2 purple yams, peeled and cubed
- 1½ tablespoons coconut oil
- 1/8 teaspoon ground cumin
- 1 tablespoon maple syrup

Preparation:

1. Preheat the oven to 350 degrees F.
2. Place potatoes, yams and carrots in a baking dish and top with ground cumin, cumin seeds, coconut oil and cayenne pepper.

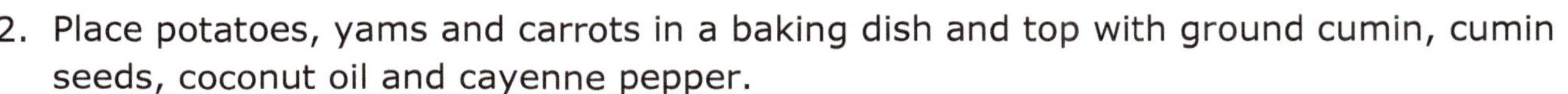

3. Toss to coat well and place the dish in baking oven.
4. Bake for about 45 minutes and take out.
5. Top with maple syrup and serve.

Serving Suggestions: Garnish with coriander before serving.

Variation Tip: Salt and black pepper can be added for better taste.

Nutritional Information per Serving:

Calories: 567 | **Fat:** 37.7g|**Sat Fat:** 32.4g|**Carbohydrates:** 57.4g|**Fiber:** 7.4g|**Sugar:** 11.4g|**Protein:** 3.4g

Thai Fried Spinach with Peanuts

Preparation Time: 5 minutes
Cooking Time: 6 minutes
Servings: 1

Ingredients:

- ½ bunch fresh spinach
- 1 tablespoon oyster sauce
- ½ tablespoon sherry
- ½ teaspoon sesame oil
- ¼ cup peanuts, chopped
- 2 garlic cloves, finely chopped
- 2 tablespoons chicken stock
- ½ tablespoon fish sauce
- ½ teaspoon brown sugar
- 1 tablespoon vegetable oil

Preparation:

1. Add chicken sauce, sesame oil, sherry, oyster sauce, fish sauce and brown sugar in a bowl. Mix well.
2. Heat up vegetable oil in a pan and add garlic in it.
3. Fry for about 1 minute and add spinach in it.
4. Stir well and add in sherry mixture after 1 minute.
5. Cook for about 4 minutes and take out.
6. Top with chopped peanuts and serve.

Serving Suggestions: Serve with red chili flakes on the top.

Variation Tip: You can also use stevia instead of sugar.

Nutritional Information per Serving:

Calories: 436 | **Fat:** 34.6g|**Sat Fat:** 5.6g|**Carbohydrates:** 16.6g|**Fiber:** 7g|**Sugar:** 4.1g|**Protein:** 15.3g

Thai Stir-Fried Mixed Vegetables

Preparation Time: 5 minutes
Cooking Time: 10 minutes
Servings: 2

Ingredients:

- 2 garlic cloves, minced
- 1 tablespoon chopped carrots
- 1 tablespoon light soy sauce
- ¼ teaspoon vegan Worcestershire sauce
- 2 tablespoons water
- ½ teaspoon vegetable oil
- ½ cup mushroom, chopped
- 6 tablespoons broccoli
- 1 tablespoon dark soy sauce
- ½ teaspoon sugar
- 1 cup white cabbage, shredded

Preparation:

1. Fry garlic in a frying pan and add mushrooms after 1 minute.
2. Add in carrots, broccoli, vegetable oil, Worcestershire sauce, soy sauce, water and sugar. Stir well.
3. Cook for around 8 minutes and add in shredded cabbage.
4. Cook for about 1 minute and take out.
5. Serve and enjoy!

Serving Suggestions: Serve with cashews on the top.

Variation Tip: You can also use almond oil instead of vegetable oil.

Nutritional Information per Serving:

Calories: 95 | **Fat:** 1.3g|**Sat Fat:** 0.2g|**Carbohydrates:** 26.5g|**Fiber:** 1.6g|**Sugar:** 19.7g|**Protein:** 3.8g

Thai Tropical Fruit Salad

Preparation Time: 7 minutes
Servings: 3

Ingredients:

- ½ cup fresh pineapple cubes
- ½ cup mango, sliced
- ½ star fruit, peeled and sliced
- 2 tablespoons coconut milk
- 1½ tablespoons coconut sugar
- ½ banana, sliced
- ½ cup lychee fruit
- 1 cup strawberries
- ½ tablespoon lime juice

Preparation:

1. Add coconut milk, lime juice and sugar in a bowl. Mix well.
2. Now, add mango, pineapple, star fruit, banana, lychee and strawberries in another bowl. Mix well.
3. Add coconut milk mixture in the fruits and toss to coat well.
4. Serve and enjoy!

Serving Suggestions: Serve with berries on the top.

Variation Tip: You can also use brown sugar.

Nutritional Information per Serving:

Calories: 277 | **Fat:** 2.8g|**Sat Fat:** 2.2g|**Carbohydrates:** 55.7g|**Fiber:** 2.8g|**Sugar:** 11.2g|**Protein:** 3.4g

Thai Rice Salad

Preparation Time: 10 minutes
Servings: 8

Ingredients:

- 3 cups long-grain rice, boiled
- 6 tablespoons fish sauce
- ½ cup sugar
- 2 cucumbers, peeled and diced
- 8 scallions, chopped
- 6 tablespoons lime juice
- 4 tablespoons cooking oil
- ¼ teaspoon cayenne
- 6 carrots, grated
- ¾ cup chopped cilantro
- Salt and black pepper, to taste

Preparation:

1. Combine rice, fish sauce, sugar, cucumbers and scallions in a large bowl.
2. Add in lime juice, oil, cayenne, carrots, salt and pepper. Mix properly.
3. Garnish with cilantro and set aside for about 5 minutes.
4. Serve and enjoy!

Serving Suggestions: You can serve with red chili flakes on the top.

Variation Tip: You can omit black pepper.

Nutritional Information per Serving:

Calories: 409 | **Fat:** 7.4g|**Sat Fat:** 1.2g|**Carbohydrates:** 79.7g|**Fiber:** 3g|**Sugar:** 17.5g|**Protein:** 6.9g

Vegan Thai Rice Salad

Preparation Time: 15 minutes
Servings: 2

Ingredients:

- ½ cup wild and brown rice mix, cooked
- ½ yellow bell pepper, chopped
- 1½ cups kale, roughly chopped
- 2 green onions, thinly sliced
- ½ red bell pepper, chopped
- 1 cup shredded purple cabbage
- ¼ cucumber, chopped
- ¼ cup cashews, roughly chopped
- 2 tablespoons low-sodium soy sauce
- 1 tablespoon sesame oil
- ½ garlic clove, minced
- ½ teaspoon chili flakes
- 1 tablespoon hoisin sauce
- 1 tablespoon rice vinegar
- ½ tablespoon freshly grated ginger

Preparation:

1. Add rice, yellow bell pepper, red bell pepper, purple cabbage, cucumber, kale and green onions in a large bowl. Mix well.
2. Meanwhile, combine soy sauce, sesame oil, garlic clove, chili flakes, hoisin sauce, rice vinegar and ginger in another bowl. Mix properly to form a smooth mixture.
3. Pour the dressing in the rice mixture and top with cashews.
4. Serve and enjoy!

Serving Suggestions: Top with lime wedges before serving.

Variation Tip: Hoisin sauce can be omitted.

Nutritional Information per Serving:

Calories: 373 | **Fat:** 15.7g|**Sat Fat:** 2.7g|**Carbohydrates:** 50.8g|**Fiber:** 6.9g|**Sugar:** 9.1g|**Protein:** 12.3g

Thai Mango Salad

Preparation Time: 12 minutes
Servings: 2

Ingredients:

- ½ Thai green mango, thinly sliced
- ½ zucchini, thinly sliced
- ½ red pepper, chopped
- 1 spring onion, finely chopped
- ½ red chili, diced finely
- 1 cup roasted peanuts, roughly chopped
- 1 tablespoon lime juice
- ½ garlic clove, pressed
- ½ teaspoon maple syrup
- ½ tablespoon sesame oil
- 1 tablespoon tamari
- Black pepper, to taste

Preparation:

1. Add mango, zucchini, red pepper, onion, and red chili in a bowl. Mix well.
2. Meanwhile, whisk lime juice, garlic clove, maple syrup, sesame oil, tamari and black pepper in another bowl.
3. Pour the dressing in the mango mixture and top with roasted peanuts.
4. Serve and enjoy!

Serving Suggestions: Serve with chopped mint leaves on the top.

Variation Tip: You can also use soy sauce to enhance taste.

Nutritional Information per Serving:

Calories: 507 | **Fat:** 39.6g|**Sat Fat:** 5.5g|**Carbohydrates:** 27.1g|**Fiber:** 8.3g|**Sugar:** 7.7g|**Protein:** 21.2g

Thai Green Papaya Salad

Preparation Time: 15 minutes
Servings: 3

Ingredients:

- 2½ tablespoons fresh lime juice
- 1½ tablespoons fish sauce
- 2 garlic cloves, minced
- ½ green papaya, peeled, halved and seeded
- ½ cup chopped fresh cilantro
- ½ Thai red chili, thinly sliced
- 1½ tablespoons palm sugar
- 1 tablespoon dried shrimp, chopped
- 5 cherry tomatoes, halved
- 1 green onion, thinly sliced
- 1 tablespoon salted peanuts, chopped

Preparation:

1. Add lime juice, sugar, fish sauce, shrimp and garlic cloves in a bowl. Whisk well.
2. Meanwhile, add papaya, tomatoes, cilantro, red chili and green onion in a bowl. Mix well.
3. Combine papaya mixture with the lime juice mixture and toss to coat well.
4. Top with salted peanuts and serve.

Serving Suggestions: Garnish with red chili flakes before serving.

Variation Tip: Use oregano to enhance taste.

Nutritional Information per Serving:

Calories: 161 | **Fat:** 2.6g|**Sat Fat:** 0.5g|**Carbohydrates:** 25.4g|**Fiber:** 3.9g|**Sugar:** 18.9g|**Protein:** 11.3g

Exquisite and Exciting Curries

Thai Lentil Chickpea Yellow Curry

Preparation Time: 7 minutes
Cooking Time: 23 minutes
Servings: 4

Ingredients:

- ¼ cup lentils
- 1 cup chickpeas
- 1 ½ tablespoons yellow curry paste
- 1 cup coconut milk
- 3 garlic cloves, peeled and chopped
- ½ onion, chopped
- Salt, to taste

Preparation:

1. Take a large skillet and fry onion and garlic in it for about 3 minutes.
2. Add in yellow curry paste, coconut milk and lentils and cook for about 15 minutes.
3. Stir in chickpeas and cook for about 5 minutes.
4. Take out and serve hot.

Serving Suggestions: Squeeze lemon in the curry before serving.

Variation Tip: You can also use cashew butter to fry onion and garlic.

Nutritional Information per Serving:

Calories: 405 | **Fat:** 20.9g|**Sat Fat:** 13g|**Carbohydrates:** 44g|**Fiber:** 15.2g|**Sugar:** 8.2g|**Protein:** 14.4g

Thai Garbanzo Curry

Cooking Time: 5 minutes
Preparation Time: 11 minutes
Servings: 2

Ingredients:

- 1 tablespoon olive oil
- 1 cup garbanzo, drained
- ½ tablespoon fish sauce
- ½ tablespoon soy sauce
- ½ onion, diced
- 1 tomato, chopped
- ¾ cup coconut milk
- 1 tablespoon brown sugar
- 2 lime leaves

Preparation:

1. Heat oil in a skillet and sauté onion in it.
2. Add in garbanzo and tomato. Stir well.
3. Cook for about 1 minute and add fish sauce, coconut milk, soy sauce and brown sugar.
4. Mix properly and cook for about 10 minutes.
5. Take out and serve with lime leaves on the top.

Serving Suggestions: Garnish with cilantro before serving.

Variation Tip: Olive oil can be replaced with almond oil.

Nutritional Information per Serving:

Calories: 467 | **Fat:** 30.1g|**Sat Fat:** 20.2g|**Carbohydrates:** 47.8g|**Fiber:** 10.1g|**Sugar:** 10.7g|**Protein:** 9.5g

Thai Butternut Squash Curry

Preparation Time: 5 minutes
Cooking Time: 16 minutes
Servings: 2

Ingredients:

- 2 tablespoons red curry paste
- 1 tablespoons yellow curry paste
- ½ cup vegetable stock
- ½ cup chopped potatoes
- ¾ cup chickpeas
- 1 tablespoon brown sugar
- ½ tablespoon vegetable oil
- ½ cup coconut milk
- ½ cup cubed butternut squash
- Salt, to taste

Preparation:

1. Heat oil in a skillet and add red and yellow curry paste in it.
2. Cook for about 1 minute and add vegetable stock, potatoes, coconut milk and squash. Stir well.
3. Cook for about 10 minutes and add in chickpeas, brown sugar, and salt.
4. Take out after 5 minutes and serve.

Serving Suggestions: Serve warm with some coriander on the top.

Variation Tip: You can also use olive oil.

Nutritional Information per Serving:

Calories: 601 | **Fat:** 31.3g|**Sat Fat:** 15.3g|**Carbohydrates:** 66.3g|**Fiber:** 17.4g|**Sugar:** 15.5g|**Protein:** 16.8g

Thai Pumpkin Curry

Preparation Time: 10 minutes
Cooking Time: 17 minutes
Servings: 2

Ingredients:

- ½ tablespoon olive oil
- 1 teaspoon curry powder
- ¾ cup coconut milk
- 3 tablespoons chopped spinach
- ½ onion, chopped
- 2 cups cubed pumpkin
- ½ cup vegetable broth
- ¼ cup cilantro, chopped

Preparation:

1. Heat oil in a pot and add onion and curry powder in it.
2. Fry for about 2 minutes and stir in pumpkin, coconut milk and broth.
3. Cook for about 10 minutes and add in spinach. Stir well.
4. Take out after 5 minutes and top with cilantro.
5. Serve and enjoy!

Serving Suggestions: Top with cashews before serving.

Variation Tip: Almond milk can be used instead of coconut milk.

Nutritional Information per Serving:

Calories: 311 | **Fat:** 25.7g|**Sat Fat:** 19.7g|**Carbohydrates:** 20.6g|**Fiber:** 5.7g|**Sugar:** 6.9g|**Protein:** 5.6g

Thai Green Curry

Preparation Time: 15 minutes
Cooking Time: 17 minutes
Servings: 8

Ingredients:

- 4 tablespoons vegetable oil
- 3½ cups coconut milk
- 2 teaspoons white sugar
- 12 lime leaves
- 4 eggplants, sliced
- 2 cups vegetable broth
- 2 teaspoons fish sauce
- 3 cups sliced chicken thighs
- 3 cups snow peas, trimmed
- 4 tablespoons green curry paste
- 4 cups chopped basil
- 2 tablespoons lime juice
- Salt, to taste

Preparation:

1. Heat up vegetable oil in a skillet and add green curry paste in it.
2. Cook for about 3 minutes and add in broth and coconut milk. Stir well.
3. Stir in fish sauce, sugar, salt, lime leaves and chicken. Cook for about 7 minutes.
4. Add in eggplants and cook for about 5 minutes.
5. Stir in basil leaves, lime juice and snow peas and cook for about 2 minutes.
6. Take out and serve.

Serving Suggestions: Squeeze lemon on the top.

Variation Tip: You can also use chicken broth.

Nutritional Information per Serving:

Calories: 1395 | **Fat:** 124.3g|**Sat Fat:** 100.9g|**Carbohydrates:** 61.5g| **Fiber:** 24.6g|**Sugar:** 29.3g|**Protein:** 32.9g

Thai Red Curry Noodles

Preparation Time: 10 minutes
Cooking Time: 10 minutes
Servings: 4

Ingredients:

- 2 cups rice noodles, soaked
- 4 garlic cloves, finely chopped
- 1 cup vegetable broth
- 2 tablespoons maple syrup
- 4 tablespoons red curry paste
- 2 cups coconut milk
- 4 tablespoons soy sauce
- 2 tablespoons lime juice
- Salt, to taste

Preparation:

1. Add red curry paste in a skillet and cook for about 5 minutes.
2. Stir in garlic and cook for about 1 minute.
3. Add in coconut milk, noodles, soy sauce, lime juice, maple syrup and vegetable broth. Mix well.
4. Cook for about 4 minutes and take out.
5. Serve and enjoy!

Serving Suggestions: Top with sesame seeds before serving.

Variation Tip: You can also add green onions to enhance taste.

Nutritional Information per Serving:

Calories: 486 | **Fat:** 33.7g|**Sat Fat:** 27g|**Carbohydrates:** 42.6g|**Fiber:** 3.8g|**Sugar:** 10.8g|**Protein:** 6g

Thai Pineapple Chicken Curry

Preparation Time: 10 minutes
Cooking Time: 50 minutes
Servings: 3

Ingredients:

- 1 cup cooked jasmine rice
- 2 tablespoons red curry paste
- 1 chicken breast, cut into strips
- 2 tablespoons white sugar
- ¼ red bell pepper, julienned
- ¼ small onion, chopped
- 2 cups water
- ¾ cup coconut milk
- 1½ tablespoons fish sauce
- ½ cup bamboo shoots, drained
- ¼ green bell pepper, julienned
- ½ cup pineapple chunks, drained

Preparation:

1. Add water and rice in a pot and cook for about 25 minutes.
2. Add in coconut milk, red curry paste, fish sauce, chicken, bamboo shoots and sugar. Stir well.
3. Cook for about 15 minutes and stir in green bell pepper, red bell pepper and onion.
4. Cook for about 10 minutes and take out.
5. Stir in pineapple chunks and serve.

Serving Suggestions: Serve with chopped minty leaves on top.

Variation Tip: You can also use oregano to enhance taste.

Nutritional Information per Serving:

Calories: 505 | **Fat:** 18.3g|**Sat Fat:** 13.7g|**Carbohydrates:** 70.6g|**Fiber:** 5.8g|**Sugar:** 16.4g|**Protein:** 15.4g

Thai Chicken Curry

Preparation Time: 10 minutes
Cooking Time: 35 minutes
Servings: 8

Ingredients:

- 3 pounds chicken breasts
- 2 red bell peppers, thinly sliced
- 4 garlic cloves, minced
- 4 tablespoons red curry paste
- 6 tablespoons torn cilantro
- 4 tablespoons coconut oil
- 1 tablespoon grated ginger
- 3½ cups coconut milk
- Salt and pepper, to taste

Preparation:

1. Preheat the oven to 375 degrees F.
2. Season chicken with pepper and salt. Set aside.
3. Meanwhile, add coconut oil and chicken in a skillet and cook until golden brown.
4. Add in garlic, pepper and ginger and cook for about 2 minutes.
5. Stir in curry paste and cook for about 5 minutes.
6. Add in coconut milk and stir well.
7. Put the skillet in the baking oven for about 25 minutes and take out.
8. Garnish with cilantro and serve.

Serving Suggestions: Top with peanuts and serve.

Variation Tip: You can also use tomatoes to enhance taste.

Nutritional Information per Serving:

Calories: 1503 | **Fat:** 132.6g|**Sat Fat:** 108.4g|**Carbohydrates:** 32g| **Fiber:** 11.5g| **Sugar:** 17.8g|**Protein:** 61.1g

Thai Beef Curry

Preparation Time: 15 minutes
Cooking Time: 90 minutes
Servings: 3

Ingredients:

- 1 pound stewing beef, cut into bite-sized pieces
- 1 tablespoon vegetable oil
- ½ tablespoon minced ginger
- 2 cups beef stock
- ½ onion, minced
- 2 garlic cloves, minced
- 2 tablespoons red curry paste
- ½ butternut squash, chopped
- 1 tablespoon lime juice
- ¾ cup coconut milk
- Salt and pepper, to taste

Preparation:

1. Season beef with pepper and salt.
2. Heat oil in a pan and add beef in it. Cook for about 5 minutes.
3. Take out and set aside.
4. Now, add ginger, garlic and onion in the pan and cook for about 5 minutes.
5. Stir in beef stock, curry paste and beef and simmer for about an hour.
6. Add in squash and cook for about 20 minutes.
7. Stir in lime juice and coconut milk and take out.
8. Serve and enjoy!

Serving Suggestions: Serve with chopped basil leaves on the top.

Variation Tip: You can also add fish sauce to enhance taste.

Nutritional Information per Serving:

Calories: 538 | **Fat:** 31.7g|**Sat Fat:** 18.3g|**Carbohydrates:** 12.4g|**Fiber:** 2.4g|**Sugar:** 3.6g|**Protein:** 49.8g

Thai Mushroom Curry

Preparation Time: 10 minutes
Cooking Time: 14 minutes
Servings: 4

Ingredients:

- 2 cups mushrooms
- 1 onion, chopped
- 1 tablespoon tomato puree
- 1 tablespoon vegetable oil
- 1 cup coconut milk
- 1 garlic clove, minced
- 1½ lemongrass stalk, chopped
- Salt, to taste

Preparation:

1. Add onion, lemongrass, garlic, tomato puree, and salt in a blender.
2. Blend until a smooth puree is formed and set aside.
3. Meanwhile, heat oil in a pan and add puree in it.
4. Cook for about 9 minutes and add in mushrooms and coconut milk.
5. Cook for about 5 minutes and take out.
6. Serve and enjoy!

Serving Suggestions: Serve with chopped coriander on the top.

Variation Tip: Add lime juice for even better taste.

Nutritional Information per Serving:

Calories: 196 | **Fat:** 17.9g|**Sat Fat:** 13.4g|**Carbohydrates:** 9.3g|**Fiber:** 2.4g|**Sugar:** 4g|**Protein:** 3g

Shrimp and Corn Cakes

Preparation Time: 15 minutes
Cooking Time: 10 minutes
Servings: 4

Ingredients:

- 2 cups sweetcorn
- 2 eggs
- 4 tablespoons chopped coriander
- 2 tablespoons soy sauce
- 2 cups all-purpose flour
- 1 cup peeled shrimp
- 6 garlic cloves, minced
- 6 tablespoons oyster sauce
- Salt and black pepper, to taste

Preparation:

1. Add coriander, shrimp, and garlic in a bowl. Mix well.
2. Now, add in eggs, flour, sweetcorn, pepper, oyster sauce, soy sauce and salt. Whisk properly.
3. Scoop out the mixture and fry it until golden brown.
4. Take out and serve.

Serving Suggestions: Serve with sweet chili sauce.

Variation Tip: Add sesame seeds to enhance the taste.

Nutritional Information per Serving:

Calories: 365 | **Fat:** 4.1g|**Sat Fat:** 1g|**Carbohydrates:** 65.5g|**Fiber:** 4g|**Sugar:** 3g|**Protein:** 17.5g

Pork on Toast

Preparation Time: 20 minutes
Cooking Time: 30 minutes
Servings: 4

Ingredients:

- 14 bread slices
- 2 tablespoons chopped coriander stalks
- 1 tablespoon soy sauce
- ½ teaspoon brown sugar
- ½ pound minced pork
- 4 garlic cloves, minced
- 1 egg
- 1 teaspoon corn flour
- 2 tablespoons coriander leaves
- Salt, to taste

Preparation:

1. Preheat the baking oven to 150 degrees F.
2. Add garlic cloves and coriander stalks in a blender. Blend well.
3. Meanwhile, add egg, and pork in a bowl. Whisk properly.
4. Add coriander paste, sugar, corn flour, salt and soy sauce in the egg mixture. Mix well.
5. Now, spread the mixture on bread slices and top each slice with coriander leaves.
6. Place the slices in baking oven and bake for about 30 minutes.
7. Take out and serve.

Serving Suggestions: Serve with a dipping sauce.

Variation Tip: You can also use palm sugar.

Nutritional Information per Serving:

Calories: 191 | **Fat:** 4.2g|**Sat Fat:** 1.3g|**Carbohydrates:** 18.2g|**Fiber:** 0.9g|**Sugar:** 1.9g|**Protein:** 19.1g

Sweet Shredded Dried Mushrooms

Preparation Time: 25 minutes
Cooking Time: 40 minutes
Servings: 4

Ingredients:

- 2 cups mushrooms, thinly sliced
- 2 tablespoons water
- 2 tablespoons sesame seeds
- 2 tablespoons palm sugar
- 2 teaspoons soy sauce
- Salt, to taste

Preparation:

1. Preheat the baking oven to 200 degrees F.
2. Arrange mushroom slices on the baking tray and place it in the oven.
3. Bake for about 30 minutes and take out.
4. Meanwhile, add water, sesame seeds, palm sugar, soy sauce and salt in a bowl. Mix well.
5. Add mushrooms in the mixture and stir well.
6. Place mushrooms again in the baking oven and bake for about 10 minutes.
7. Take out and serve.

Serving Suggestions: Top with maple syrup before serving.

Variation Tip: Soy sauce can be replaced with fish sauce.

Nutritional Information per Serving:

Calories: 43 | **Fat:** 2.3g|**Sat Fat:** 0.3g|**Carbohydrates:** 4.4g|**Fiber:** 0.9g|**Sugar:** 2.6g|**Protein:** 2.1g

Fried Turmeric Pork Fillet

Preparation Time: 15 minutes
Cooking Time: 10 minutes
Servings: 4

Ingredients:

- 1 pound sliced pork fillet
- 10 garlic cloves, minced
- 1 teaspoon black peppercorn
- 2 tablespoons fresh turmeric
- Salt, to taste

Preparation:

1. Add turmeric root, garlic cloves, black peppercorn, and salt in a blender.
2. Blend until a smooth mixture is formed and take it out in a bowl.
3. Add pork fillets in the mixture and marinade them.
4. Set aside for about 30 minutes and fry pork fillets until golden brown.
5. Take out and serve.

Serving Suggestions: Top it with red chili sauce before serving.

Variation Tip: Add black cumin to enhance taste.

Nutritional Information per Serving:

Calories: 289 | **Fat:** 14.8g|**Sat Fat:** 5.5g|**Carbohydrates:** 5g|**Fiber:** 1g|**Sugar:** 0.2g|**Protein:** 32.4g

Shrimp and Sprouts Savory Stir Fry

Preparation Time: 10 minutes
Cooking Time: 5 minutes
Servings: 4

Ingredients:

- 2 cups Brussels sprouts, halved
- 4 garlic cloves, finely chopped
- 2 tablespoons fish sauce
- 2 tablespoons soy sauce
- 2 cups peeled shrimp
- 4 tablespoons oyster sauce
- 2 teaspoons sugar

Preparation:

1. Boil Brussels sprouts in a pan and take out.
2. Heat oil in a pan and add garlic cloves and sprouts in it.
3. Fry for about 2 minutes and add shrimp, fish sauce, soy sauce, oyster sauce and sugar in it.
4. Fry for 2 more minutes and take out.
5. Serve and enjoy!

Serving Suggestions: Top with chopped coriander before serving.

Variation Tip: You can also use vinegar to enhance taste.

Nutritional Information per Serving:

Calories: 91 | **Fat:** 0.9g|**Sat Fat:** 0.3g|**Carbohydrates:** 9g|**Fiber:** 1.8g|**Sugar:** 3.5g|**Protein:** 12.4g

Thai Shrimp Cake

Preparation Time: 10 minutes
Cooking Time: 8 minutes
Servings: 2

Ingredients:

- ½ cup breadcrumbs
- 1 tablespoon minced green onion
- 1 teaspoon fish sauce
- ¾ teaspoon minced ginger
- 1 egg
- ¼ pound shrimp, peeled, deveined and chopped
- 2 tablespoons dried coconut
- 1 tablespoon fresh cilantro, chopped
- 1 tablespoon sriracha sauce
- ½ teaspoon lime juice
- ½ garlic clove, minced
- ½ tablespoon olive oil

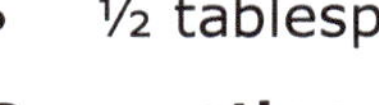

Preparation:

1. Add breadcrumbs, coconut, onion, cilantro, fish sauce, sriracha sauce, ginger, lime juice, egg, and garlic clove in a bowl. Mix well.
2. Stir in shrimp and make 2 equal balls out of the mixture.
3. Press the balls and fry them in a skillet for about 4 minutes on each side.
4. Take out and serve.

Serving Suggestions: Serve with lime wedges on top.

Variation Tip: Sriracha sauce can be replaced with hot chili sauce.

Nutritional Information per Serving:

Calories: 312 | **Fat:** 14.8g|**Sat Fat:** 4g|**Carbohydrates:** 23.7g|**Fiber:** 1.9g|**Sugar:** 3.1g|**Protein:** 19.8g

Thai Fermented Sour Sausage

Preparation Time: 15 minutes
Cooking Time: 30 minutes
Servings: 2

Ingredients:

- ½ pound minced pork
- ½ cup steamed rice
- ½ tablespoon ground black pepper
- ½ garlic head, minced
- Salt, to taste

Preparation:

1. Add pork, garlic, rice, salt and pepper in a bowl. Mix properly.
2. Make ball shapes from the mixture and place them in a zip lock bag.
3. Leave the meat to ferment for about 72 hours at room temperature.
4. Take out the meat and arrange it on skewers.
5. Grill for about 30 minutes and serve.

Serving Suggestions: Serve with chilies on the top.

Variation Tip: Cayenne pepper can be used to enhance taste.

Nutritional Information per Serving:

Calories: 336 | **Fat:** 4.3g|**Sat Fat:** 1.5g|**Carbohydrates:** 38.3g|**Fiber:** 1g|**Sugar:** 0.1g|**Protein:** 33.2g

Thai Sweet and Sour Tofu

Preparation Time: 5 minutes
Cooking Time: 25 minutes
Servings: 2

Ingredients:

- ¾ cup tofu, drained, pressed and sliced
- 1½ scallions, chopped
- 1 bell pepper, chopped
- 2 tablespoons tapioca flour
- 2½ tablespoons water
- ½ tablespoon tamari
- 1½ tablespoons brown sugar
- 1½ tablespoons rice vinegar
- ½ tablespoon ketchup
- ¼ teaspoon red pepper flakes

Preparation:

1. Add water, vinegar, tamari, ketchup, sugar and red pepper flakes in a bowl. Mix well.
2. Add tofu in the mixture and toss to coat well.
3. Fry tofu in a skillet and add scallion, bell pepper, and flour in it. Stir well.
4. Cook for about 25 minutes and take out.
5. Serve and enjoy!

Serving Suggestions: Serve with sesame seeds on the top.

Variation Tip: You can also add honey for a better taste.

Nutritional Information per Serving:

Calories: 607 | **Fat:** 4.2g|**Sat Fat:** 0.8g|**Carbohydrates:** 125.7g|**Fiber:** 3.8g|**Sugar:** 29.5g|**Protein:** 9.7g

Thai Candied Peanuts

Preparation Time: 10 minutes
Cooking Time: 25 minutes
Servings: 6

Ingredients:

- 2 cups peanuts
- 2 teaspoons cocoa powder
- ½ cup coconut milk
- 1½ cups sugar
- 2 teaspoons coffee
- ½ cup water
- 4 tablespoons sesame seeds, toasted
- Salt, to taste

Preparation:

1. Add water, sugar, cocoa powder, salt, coffee and coconut milk in a large pan. Mix well.
2. Boil the mixture and add peanuts in it.
3. Cook for about 25 minutes and take out.
4. Garnish with sesame seeds and refrigerate for 2 hours.
5. Serve and enjoy!

Serving Suggestions: Serve with maple syrup on top.

Variation Tip: Chocolate syrup can be used to enhance taste.

Nutritional Information per Serving:

Calories: 1045 | **Fat:** 31.8g|**Sat Fat:** 8g|**Carbohydrates:** 194g|**Fiber:** 5.5g|**Sugar:** 186g|**Protein:** 14.2g

Thai Sesame Peanut Brittle

Preparation Time: 19 minutes
Cooking Time: 20 minutes
Servings: 8

Ingredients:

- ½ cup granulated sugar
- ¾ cup toasted peanuts, chopped
- 2 tablespoons water
- ½ tablespoon vinegar
- ¼ cup sesame seeds, toasted
- Salt, to taste

Preparation:

1. Add sugar, water and vinegar in a pan and cook for about 12 minutes.
2. When the syrup gets hard, add sesame seeds and peanuts and mix well.
3. Place the syrup on a baking sheet lined with parchment paper and flatten it with the help of rolling pin.
4. Cut the mixture in rectangles and serve.

Serving Suggestions: Top with maple syrup before serving.

Variation Tip: Vinegar can be replaced with lemon juice.

Nutritional Information per Serving:

Calories: 150 | **Fat:** 9g|**Sat Fat:** 1.3g|**Carbohydrates:** 15.8g|**Fiber:** 1.7g|**Sugar:** 13.1g|**Protein:** 4.3g

Conclusion

Thai food can be easily found in America; however, it is considered relatively complex to prepare at homes. The reason is regarded as the unfamiliar ingredients and cooking techniques that are the peculiar property of Thai cuisine. Thai food is further divided into four categories on geographical segmentation, i.e., North, Northeastern (Isaan), Central, and Southern. Every region has its own unique taste, which will make you fall in love with it. The Thai food cookbook provides you with different recipes for various occasions, including daily meals, beverages, and desserts to understand and feel Thai cuisine at home. The cookbook will work as a bridge between you and your vacation dream of visiting Thailand and experiencing its rich culture and fantastic food.

www.ingramcontent.com/pod-product-compliance
Ingram Content Group UK Ltd.
Pitfield, Milton Keynes, MK11 3LW, UK
UKHW052226270726
14059UKWH00003B/135

9 781801 216258